# Mudville

# MUDVILLE

## STEVEN J. BINGEL

authorHOUSE®

AuthorHouse™ LLC
1663 Liberty Drive
Bloomington, IN 47403
www.authorhouse.com
Phone: 1-800-839-8640

This is a work of fiction. All of the characters, names, incidents, organizations, and dialogue in this novel are either the products of the author's imagination or are used fictitiously.

Published by AuthorHouse  09/18/2014

ISBN: 978-1-4969-3133-7 (sc)
ISBN: 978-1-4969-3132-0 (e)

Library of Congress Control Number: 2014914467

Any people depicted in stock imagery provided by Thinkstock are models, and such images are being used for illustrative purposes only.
Certain stock imagery © Thinkstock.

This book is printed on acid-free paper.

# CONTENTS

The author currently resides in Norwich, VT with his wife Maureen Chase-Bingel. They have a large family of seven children and two grandchildren. Steven attended the University of New Hampshire after separating from the United States Air Force in 1990. He studied Wildlife Management and worked for the U.S. Fish and Wildlife Service after graduation.

He has published numerous stories in The Green Mountain Trading Post, articles for his Company's quarterly Newsletter and several internet based websites. Steven also has a passion for quantum physics, and is working on a second book aptly titled: Learning To Survive in Infinity. He currently works at West Lebanon Feed & Supply in West Lebanon, N.H.. He has been there for twenty years and plans an early retirement in 2019. Steven is an avid hunter and fisherman. At the age of 52 he is finally learning to play guitar. In the winter he can be found playing ice-hockey. In his spare time he writes...

# MUDVILLE

There was a pond in my childhood called Millville. Often referred to by us kids as Mudville because of the yearly draining that revealed it's mucky bottom. Perhaps twenty-five or thirty acres of lily-pads and old stumps, it was a veritable fish heaven. Even a budding twelve year old angler could do minor damage to the bass population with a six-inch plastic worm. Purple always worked best.

Occasionally, on a hot summer evening, Pinky would accompany me to it's fertile waters. We'd walk a half mile by blacktop then continue the last quarter mile on dirt road. Our favorite spot was a sandy point that jutted out into the pond from a small grove of white pines. We simply rolled up our jeans and waded the shallow point.

This particular time, as shadows lengthened, the day was replaced by the steady chugging of jitterbugs on the calm surface. It was Pinky's favorite way to fish for bass.

Now, you never fish a jitterbug by sight, even on a moonlit night. The trick is not to react, if that's possible, when a loud splash, equivalent to a 200 pound man falling into the pond indicates a strike, and only setting the hook when you feel the fish. To say the least, it's as risky as maintaining a cholesterol level of four hundred. By night's end your nerves are shot.

Pinky would maybe miss the first strike, giving in to jitterbug-jitters, but by the second one he'd recovered. For me it was impossible. I always yanked the thing at the splash part.

However, on the night I caught the twenty-dollar fish, I must have gotten lucky. You see, Pinky and I had a long standing bet. If ever I caught a bigger bass than his of seven pounds, he'd give me twenty dollars.

My fishing gear in those newspaper-route days consisted of a Zebco closed face reel and rod combo purchased from K-Mart. It worked well on the spawning spring suckers that ran in the Hitty-Titty brook next to our house. I went through a rod for each week they were running. Anything over one pound would be questionable on it's like though'.

Wading out to the edge of deeper water, I heaved the jitterbug out as far as my gear would allow. This was about ten feet, accompanied by the usual bird-nest tangle of line. Almost immediately a fish engulfed it. I worked furiously to unravel the tangle, stepping into deep water in the process. The fish took off.

Pinky still kids me about it today.

"Funniest damn thing I ever seen…twelve year old kid barefoot water skiing without a boat….".

I pulled off a beautiful two-point landing down the shore a ways that the best Busch Gardens water-skier would have applauded, and managed to land the eight pound bass to boot.

On the walk home Pinky handed me a crisp twenty.

"Heck I've laid down more money for less entertainment than I've had tonight…" he said.

My face beamed brighter than the full moon hanging above the pines.

Millville was often a source of entertainment. In the summer, news that it was being drained would spread like wildfire through the neighborhood.

I always knew first. The Hitty-Titty brook that drained Millville ran beside our house, and it would swell and overflow it's banks into our yard, much to my delight and my Father's dismay. It was an event we kids looked forward to every summer. There was never any warning, they just opened the dam and drained the pond, regardless of the havoc it created downstream. I would go through fifteen pairs of K-Mart Huskies jeans during the week it happened. All the boys did. K-Mart would stock up just for the event. Some mid-west towns close for deer season, our's for the draining of Millville.

One such summer Pinky and I were on a small, grassy island midstream of the brook fishin' for catfish. There was a deep hole created by a beaver dam on the downstream side. We would wade the shallow side to access it.

We still argue 'bout it, but Pinky claims he was the first to notice.

"Water's rising…they must be drainin' ol' Mudville" he said.

Our escape route to safety was quickly cut off by rapidly rising water. Then the Redfern's plastic wading pool came floating by, and we made a jump for it.

It was a wild ride, especially when I forgot to duck at the culvert that ran underneath the street in front of our house. Some three miles downstream we reached a quiet back-water swamp and slogged to shore.

After a couple more runs we got bored and headed for Mudville. As usual word had quickly gotten around. All the Haigh School sixth-graders were there, clad in Huskies jeans. K-Mart would make a killin' this year. Even some of the eighth-graders had ditched girlfriends to partake in this auspicious event.

"Nice welt…" said Spider pointing to my forehead.

"Ain't it though'", Pinky chimed, "you should 'a seen that ol' pool spin when that culvert caught his head, man, we were out'a control, what a blast!".

Spider was introducing his kid brother, Eddie to his first draining. He was throwing pennies ever further out into the ooze. Eddie would run out and pick them up. About the fifth toss he just disappeared. He never screamed, mainly 'cause his mouth was full of muck. Now we knew how far we could go out.

The pond was nearly drained. All that remained was the old river bed winding through the middle of it to the dam. A state fisheries biologist had strung a gill-net across it and employed a few eager boys to wade the river and herd it's contents into the net.

It was about then that someone noticed the whirlpool near the dam. It was six feet across and thirstily sucking the remaining pond water, spewing it out in a jet on the other side to a pool many feet below.

Pinky kicked a stick into the water and we all watched it float toward the whirlpool. It went around and around until it disappeared. We all ran to the other side. Out it shot, landing in the pool below.

"Hot dog!" exclaimed Spider.

"Just like Niagara Falls!" yelled Pinky.

"We've got to get a barrel and someone's got to try it" he further stated.

A hush fell on the small gathering.

"Put them right up there with the first man on the moon" he said.

He looked at us all. Everyone averted their eyes, busy swatting at invisible mosquitoes.

"O.K. we'll do it the fair way…scissors, paper, rock" said Pinky.

Now, for those of you unfamiliar with this little game, let me fill you in. It consists of two fellas' facing each other with their right hands extended out in front of themselves balled up in a fist. To the chant of "scissors…paper…rock" in unison, they shake their fists up and down. Upon saying "rock", they either keep their hand balled up, display the index and middle finger, or thumb and all four fingers. A balled fist represents rock; two fingers-scissors and thumb and remaining four fingers-paper.

Rock crushes scissors, but is covered by paper. Scissors cut paper, but is crushed by rock.

This is done three times in succession with two wins winning the round.

Eddie was too young and Spider volunteered to round up a pickle barrel and football helmet for the lucky winner. That left Pinky and I.

We didn't call him Pinky for nothing. His right hand consisted of only one finger-his pinky. It never hampered his fishing though'. The best he could possibly manage was paper or rock, to which I would parlay paper every time and either cover his rock or tie his paper, and we'd have to shoot again.

It was a sure bet. I smugly agreed to the duel.

Oh, did I mention the players closing their eyes while doing this? Prevents cheating you know...

We faced off.

"Scissors...paper...rock" we both chanted.

I threw my paper.

Imagine my surprise when I opened my eyes and...there was his left hand with index finger and middle finger extended.

"Ha! Scissors cuts paper!" he barked.

The barrel was a little cramped, but if I cocked my football-helmet laden head sideways, it fit okay. They nailed on the cover and shoved me off. A bet's a bet.

Next day at school while all the kids were signing my cast, I recounted the story over and over.

Not once did my buddies complain 'bout the pickle smell. That's how friends are.

Then there was the time.....

# TREE TOP LAUGHTER

When you're a kid you do a lot of stupid things. It surprised my Mother that I ever made it to my tenth birthday. My Father was making bets with the guys at his office that I wouldn't. I was a long-shot, forty-to-one if I remember correctly. I even overheard one of their conversations one hot, summer day. My Father was leaning on the lawnmower sipping iced tea and talking to the neighbor, Mr. Marson.

"That boy of yours, swell kid, but a little rambunctious...." said Mr. Marson.

"Yeah, he's handful alright, lucky he survived the beehive caper" said my Father, "he'll be lucky to make it to his tenth birthday".

He further extrapolated.... "Yup, odds are rising daily, forty-to-one right now, want a piece of the action?".

Mr. Marson said "forty-to-one huh?, sure why not, way he's going sounds like easy money".

So it was. Sure I did a lot of stupid things like I said. We all did at that age. We all thought we were invincible (although I had to look up it's meaning in Webster's dictionary). One of the more brilliant ideas I ....I mean Frankie Green and his brother Richie ever came up with was the Stop Sign Robbery.

My folks had just bought their first home and the mortgage was pretty steep. So, my Father worked his full-time job and a part-time job, and my Mother worked part-time also to help ends meet. The good that came of it all was that I got to spend many weekends at my Grandmother's house on Country Pond. Life with my Grandmother was easier than that with my parents. She understood the internal yearning of a rambunctious nine-year old. All I wanted to do was explore, sleep out under the stars and fish from the dock all night, to catch fireflies, and seek out the deep-throated bullfrog that always called from the swamp on the opposite side of the road. I always obeyed my Grandmother (mainly because she always let me do what I wanted). This was something that seemed to amaze my Mother when she came to pick me up on Sunday night.

"I don't know how you do it Daisy, he won't listen to a thing I say!" she would always exclaim.

That is until I hooked-up with Frankie Green and his kid brother, Richie.

It was Friday night, my Mother had barely cleared the driveway when I hit-up Gram.

"How about letting me sleep out in the yard in my tent Nana?" I asked.

"Okay" she said.

Just like that. Piece of cake!.

I set about erecting the tent and rigging my pole for the night's fishing. I was pounding in the last stake when a voice asked;

"Whatcha' doin'?".

I swung around and faced an oversized eight-year old kid, busy digging for something in his nose.

"Putting up my tent, what's it look like" I said turning back to the stake.

"Are you gonna' sleep in it?" he asked.

"Course I'm gonna' sleep in it stupid!" I replied. What did he think I was going to do?

"All night?" he inquired.

"Yeah, all night!" I said. My anger was welling up.

He placed whatever he'd been digging for into his mouth and licked his finger with great satisfaction.

"Could I sleep in it too?" he asked.

"I don't think so" I replied. Then I thought up a quick scheme to get rid of him.

"Haven't you ever heard of the little green man that lives in the swamp across the road?. He comes prowling at night, and just might decide to investigate this here tent. Who knows what could happen? Why, the last kid that saw him still hasn't regained his eyesight yet".

The kid's eyes were getting wider and wider. He even stopped the excavation, his finger pointing straight up in silent ready.

"Richeeee!" a voice beckoned. "Suppertime!, come in and get washed up!".

I never saw him leave, only a spray of gravel where he once stood. I snickered to myself, "works every time", and went back to work on the finishing touches to my tent. Another voice interrupted me. I turned angrily to really put the fear of God into him, only it was a different kid.

"You seen my kid brother?, he's gotta' come in and eat" he said.

"He's already eaten" I said mocking with my finger up my nose.

"Yeah, that's my brother, we call him Nose, say that an Arbogast jitterbug?" he asked.

I followed his gaze to my pole.

"Sure is, you like to fish" I asked.

"Sure, only we don't get to too much on account we live in the city, and only come here for a week during summer vacation" he said.

"Well, I'm sleeping out and fishing all night, want to come?" I asked.

"I don't know if my Mom will let me, but I'll ask, see you after supper!" he said. He turned and ran back to the summer cottage two places over.

"Frankie Green" he said in response to my question later that night. We were unfurling our sleeping bags, mindful not to squash the Twinkies and a six-pack of pop his Mom had provided. Unfortunately, Nose had accompanied him. One of his Mom's stipulations "You have to take your brother along" things.

"We're from…." began Frankie.

"Min-e-apples" chimed Nose.

"That's Minneapolis stupid" said Frankie

"My Dad rents the cottage for a week every summer. Only time we get to fish. He's always away in Boston working, but my Mom's here with us. He says it's a good change of environment for us" said Frankie.

"Yeah on account we get into so much trouble at home" said Nose.

He was busy at work in the left nostril this time. Oh well, at least he switched off.

"Wanna' go fishin'" I asked.

"You bet!" said Frankie and Nose in unison.

About two o'clock in the morning the fish quit biting. We were sitting on the end of the dock, bare feet dangling in the warm water. Occasionally one of us would flip his jitterbug up in the air and watch the bats swoop at it, until Nose hooked one and fell in trying to reel it in. Funniest thing I ever seen. He could even swim with one arm, the other securely stuck to his nose with one finger inserted.

"So what do you do for excitement in Minneapolis?" I asked Frankie.

(Little did I know that by asking that simple question that I would almost fulfill my Father's prophecy and make him a rich man).

What Nose lacked in bat-fishing ability, he made up for in stealth and mechanical prowess. He had the stop sign off the pole with blinding speed and ran with it, only tripping once, to Frankie and I hiding in the bushes.

"Now what do we do with it?" I asked.

"I don't know" said Frankie.

"Sure is a beauty though', no bullet holes like the ones we got back home" said Nose.

We all sat admiring the shiny, red stop sign, unsure what to do next.

"I got it!" said Frankie snapping his fingers.

"We'll take it to the old culvert at the entrance to the grove" he further stated.

"Then what?" asked Nose.

"Well, we….we…." Frankie looked at me for inspiration.

But they were the brains of the operation, and I could offer no input.

"We set it up in the middle of the road and get some toilet paper and string that across the bridge and stop cars!" he blurted it all out in one breath.

"At three o'clock in the morning?" I reminded him.

"Sure, it'll be a gas!" said Frankie.

I doubted his judgment, but Nose seemed eager, so I went along with it.

"Okay, but let me do it!" I said.

After getting it all in place we realized there was no place to hide. The only cover was a skimpy pine tree about eight inches in diameter next to the culvert. It would have to do. So we all shimmied up, myself last, pushing Nose from below as Frankie tugged on his free arm because the other was busy.

No sooner had we gotten in place when…headlights! Our first victim! We could barely contain our snickering and chortling.

The car eased up to the stop sign, and just sat there with it's headlights illuminating the bright red paint.

"What's he doing?" whispered Frankie.

"Don't know" I replied.

Seconds drug into an eternity. Still the car sat idling.

"Well, I'm going down" said Frankie.

He proceeded down the tree.

"Ouch, watch the fingers!" yelled Nose.

Yeah, I thought, like a surgeon's hands, or a pianist's fingers, you don't want to mess with his livelihood.

Frankie dropped to the ground, and tucked and rolled into the shadows. He crept up the bank and onto the asphalt behind the car.

"What are you doing?" I whispered.

He shrugged his shoulders in silent response. Then he pointed to the trunk and made the sign for okay with his fingers. Not quite sure what he meant, I signed okay back. Then all hell broke loose. In the blink of an eye with an Indian war whoop that would have put Geronimo to shame, he jumped on to the trunk and banged his fists up and down.

The car that had been idling came to life, and with a screech of tires and burning rubber it shot through the makeshift roadblock sending Frankie scrambling for his life. He dove for the bank, but misjudged. The railing caught his ankle and he fell into the culvert with a loud splash.

Nose and I laughed so hard that the tree started swaying back and forth out over the water, and with a loud wood-splitting noise, broke off just below our feet. One minute we were snug in the pine tree, next we were all treading water. Frankie and Nose were laughing their heads off between drowning.

"Man, did you see that guy take off!" said Frankie.

"Some fun, huh?" said Nose.

"Sure" I gurgled, spitting Pickerel weed from between my teeth, "what else do you guys do for excitement?".

# SUMMER RAIN

I was holding my breath trying to apply the final coat of cement to the lime and chartreuse grasshopper when something distracted me. What was that sound? Rain. Not just any rain, but a cleansing, life-renewing, summer rain.

I pushed myself from the table and went to the door. The soft glow of the porch light revealed silvery-thin pencils of rain. Steam was rising from the sidewalk. I could smell the azaleas, fresh and wet in their June colors. Little mounds of rich, brown loam lie in herald to the presence of night crawlers in the moist grass. Some lay stranded in puddles, wriggling helplessly.

I glanced at the street and noticed a stranger clad in overcoat and hat strolling leisurely through the rain. He stopped in the glare of the streetlight and did a little jig in one of the puddles, kicking water with his galoshes. He was enjoying himself, and for a moment I was envious, and wished I were he. I basked in his joy. He then recomposed himself as if aware he was being watched, and walked on.

To my surprise, when he reached my walk, he turned and headed toward my house. His collar was pulled up tight, and his hat sat low on his brow. His face was hidden in it's shadow. When he reached the comfort of the porch light, he looked up, and then I recognized him. I should have guessed. Only an old, dyed-in-the-wool fisherman such as he would be out on a night like this. He was out in the rain like a hungry trout on the prowl. I opened the screen door and offered to take his dripping hat and slicker, warning him to remove his galoshes, 'lest he muddy the freshly scrubbed floor and face the wrath of my wife. She would hang us both out to dry.

His face was aglow and his eyes snapped and twinkled. As he rolled his cigar from cheek to cheek with his tongue, I removed wet socks and admonished them to newspaper next to the stove. I replaced them with my slippers, and placed a blanket over his gaunt frame. I had learned not to rush him, and insured he was dry and comfortably seated at the table with a mug of steaming-hot coffee and fresh baked ginger snap cookies before gently prodding him for his sudden, unexpected (but always welcome) appearance at my door.

"Was I aware", he started, "that a man could spend his entire life, inside, in the relative comfort of his home, never venturing forth except for the occasional tobacco from the corner store".

He huffed.

"Just sitting at the kitchen table, wasting his time tying flies", he said eyeing the grasshopper and waggled a finger in my face.

"Besides, you got that thing all wrong! Ain't no trout in the world gonna eat a grasshopper with five legs!" he lamented.

After bestowing me with his intimate knowledge of grasshoppers, I looked at the fly and to my astonishment discovered he was right! I guess I'd been daydreaming and had inadvertently tied on a fifth leg.

"Now any smart trout knows on a night like this with a good summer rain coming down that there's food to be had" Pinky said.

He had a point. I envisioned the as-of-late dry river. It would be near overflowing it's banks. The trout would be out and active over the next few days. The rain would bring respite from the thus far, dry summer. The water would become cooler and the trout would feel invigorated.

13

They would leave the undercut banks, seeking morsels loosened by the new rain. It was like ringing the dinner bell.

I also briefly thought about the screens I promised my wife I would wash.

"Not me", he continued his sermon, as if aware of my predicament.

"I've been feeling the tug of this rain since my corn began throbbing last Tuesday, I knew it was gonna' rain" said Pinky. He had removed his slipper and was wiggling his big toe.

I tipped the coffee pot to refill his cup, never taking my eyes from him. I was hooked and he was slowly reeling me in. He delivered the coup' de grace.

"No sireee…not me, on a night like this you wouldn't find me fiddling around tying flies, nope, I'd be out on the river trying for one of those big browns" he said quite animated.

I'd heard enough. All the dirty screens in the county couldn't stop me now.

"So when do we leave?" I asked.

"Thought you'd see it my way", he almost smiled. Instead, he bit the end off his stogie and spat it out the door.

"See you at my place in five minutes" he said.

And he was gone. I was left quivering and tingly, not sure what to do next.

As I slipped on waders, hat and mosquito dope, my wife appeared, hands on hips and quipped;

"It was him, he was here, right? Talked you right into going fishing didn't he? What about the dirty screens?" she inquired.

I gave her my best fish-out-of-water expression.

"Tomorrow?" I pleaded.

She threw her hands up and stormed toward the refrigerator.

"Well, at least let me make you a sandwich and some coffee" she said.

Moments later she stuffed the paper sack and thermos into my already overloaded arms. I kissed her cheek lightly as I passed.

"Don't forget, you promised, tomorrow!" she yelled as I scurried towards Pinky's house. I skinned my shin on a carelessly placed wheelbarrow, just one of the hazards of the sport. Makes you feel less ashamed when you have to endure some pain. I just wish I hadn't broke the tip off from that split-bamboo fly rod in the process.

Pinky sat clenching the steering wheel in the already running car, it's back seat filled with various paraphernalia. Just for a split second I thought I'd been had. But, in his sovereign wisdom, Pinky rebuked.

"What took ya' so long?" he huffed.

I stammered.

"Well, I...I...some fool left a wheelbarrow on my front lawn and I...."

"Never mind, climb in and don't get the new upholstery all wet!" he said.

I barely managed to get seated before the car abruptly lurched down the driveway and into the wet night.

As we sped down the old, familiar road, with windows rolled up, Pinky extolled on the virtues of air conditioning and power steering, all the comforts and gadgets of modern technology. The drive was short and soon the headlights shone on coarse gravel as we turned off the main road. The going got bumpy, and once we almost got stuck, but with a little coaxing and a few explicative words Pinky kept making progress. At just the right fork in the road he cranked the wheel hard, and we skidded to a gravel-spewing halt. When he switched off the ignition the air conditioning stopped also and the humid June air quickly found it's way into the car's interior. I could hear the peepers, and ever so quietly, the whisper of running water.

"You go on ahead" I told him, knowing he would be eager to get on the river.

"I just want to sit here a minute" I added.

"Wanna' play nature boy again, eh?" he chortled.

"Something like that" I said.

"Just don't fall asleep nature boy" he gruffed.

He disappeared in the gently falling rain. Although he had a flashlight like myself, he knew the way and preferred to walk without it's guiding beam.

"Might scare the fish" he would say.

I loved him, although I would never discuss such sentiments face to face.

The rain hissed as it fell through the pines overhead. Somewhere in the dark a whippoorwill called. I wanted to capture the moment, store it away for some later time.

I was brought back to reality by a light tapping on the glass. It was Pinky.

I'd been caught.

"You gonna' sit there all night dilly-dallying or what? There's fish to be had!" he hollered.

I searched his face and suddenly I understood; he was worried. He had gotten to the river, fished for awhile then realized I wasn't present. Gotten worried and come back to check on me, hadn't he? I implied.

"Nothing of the sort, just forgot my bug dope" he replied.

He pretended to rummage through the back seat, oblivious to me.

Was this the same man who when I tipped the canoe over right after ice-out, and while standing there shivering with our tobacco all wet, offered me a drink from his thermos, and then chuckled at me when I drank it and discovered it was ice water?

He had been worried.

"Where's that darn stuff gotten off to!" he snorted.

"Here use mine" I said.

He palmed the bottle, squirted a little into his hand and gingerly patted his neck, never looking directly at me.

"What!" he suddenly yelled.

"You gonna' sit there gawking at me, or are we going fishing?" he asked.

I reveled in triumph. I donned my slicker and we walked down the path toward the river, not speaking a word. A hundred feet from the bank he called a halt to our approach.

"Gotta' study the water, sneak up on 'em, don't want every fish from here to Clark County hear you with your fool bumbling" he said.

He set the pace from here, tip-toeing slowly, sometimes balanced on one foot, while the other searched for twigs that would betray our presence.

Once, I almost slipped on the slick pine needles, but a piercing glance from Pinky put me in my place. I was more careful from there on.

At the bank, he assumed a commando-like crawl with me following suit. After all, this man could catch trout-big trout-in a summer rain puddle. He was a fish God and I, a meager subservient.

He slid into the water without a ripple. It was as though two friends were embracing after a long separation. The river and he became one.

"See you in an hour" he said over his back stripping line from his reel. He headed upstream. I watched him go until he rounded the bend and disappeared from view.

I waded in and slowly felt my way along the rock strewn bottom. I headed downstream. As Pinky had predicted, the fish were voraciously feeding. Although I could not see them, I could hear them slapping the surface as they fed. One particularly large *plop!* caught my attention. I swiveled my head around to determine the general location of it's signature splash. In one of those magical moments that can only happen on a night such as this, the clouds parted and a swath of moonlight bathed the river. The fish rose again, and I caught a glimpse of his pale form as he cleared the water. What a fish! My hands began to shake. I stripped line and started a slow roll cast, gingerly setting the fly down upstream of him. When it was over his window I gently shook the rod-tip and imparted a tantalizing quiver to the fly. The water bulged underneath it, then caved in as if someone had pulled the plug on the bottom of the river. My fly disappeared in the void. At the same instant my rod came to life, and I realized he was hooked! No one had told the fish yet. He must have turned sideways to return to his little niche in the river when he felt the resistance. Then he switched gears from first to afterburner in the blink of an eye. He ran at an angle upstream, then turned, leaving me taking up slack line as fast as I could. If he had been hard to control against the current, he was downright impossible running with it. I had all I could do just to run along the water's edge to stay with him. The line sliced the water and hummed. I didn't know how much more it would endure. Then he stopped. No reason. Just stopped, mid-stream in a deep pool, and shook his head. The line transmitted each twist to my aching hands. It was a good sign, he was tired. Now I had time to breathe, ease up a little and gain a few precious inches of line. I walked slowly downstream of his position, careful to keep the line taught. When I felt comfortable I began applying pressure to move him. He must have gotten his second wind, because off he went again. This time he jumped. Three times. Each time I felt him coming up I laid the rod horizontal to the water and prayed. He shook each time his head broke the surface as if he were some crazy terrier with a rag clenched in his teeth. I swear I heard him growl. Then he tired for real. I could feel the difference. He was exhausted from the duel(as was I). Ever so gently I began reeling him in. The battle and current had taken it's toll. He was spent. I unclipped the small wooden net from my belt with my left hand while holding the rod high in the air with my right. I guided him headlong into it then realized; he wasn't going to fit! He was magnificent. A fitting adversary. I clipped the net back to my belt. I admired for but a second. Although only eighteen inches, he was fat and healthy. Not a stocked fish, but a native brown, hatched and nourished to adulthood by the river. He was creamy white and olive with dark spots that ran dorsally to his wide tail.

The fly was hand-tied, with a barbless hook, and I easily removed it from his jaw. He sensed his freedom and was gone with an indignant slap of his tail, spraying me with water. I decided to give my now racing heart a break, and waded to the bank. Pinky would be along any time now, and an old, cut-off stump under an overhanging cedar limb would provide a front row seat to the show.

The river glowed in the mixture of rain and intermittent moonlight. Undaunted by the shower, bats swooped and wheeled about close enough that I could feel their delicate wings brush my hat brim. The fish were still actively feeding also. An owl hooted mournfully behind me, and another answered from somewhere on the opposite bank. The stage was set.

From out of the swirling mist Pinky appeared. Just a ghostly outline at first, like some spirit fisherman, forever banished to eternally wade the river. His form solidified as he drew closer. He was patiently working each riffle and eddy.

"Gotta' work for those browns" he always said.

He was a master. I watched him. Arms, hands and fingers all worked in harmonious coordination. The rod was an extension of himself. Only he could have found it handy to have born with a fly rod for an arm. His casts were fluid and graceful. He preferred an eight foot rod, split bamboo with a cork handle, not like the foam ones on the market today. I found even my seven foot rod to be cumbersome with the many overhanging trees on this river. I spent as much time unsnagging flies from them as I did fishing.

"No sireee….won't catch me using any puny, pool-stick-of-a-fly-rod on this river" he once commented.

"Hey nature boy…" he yelled from the river.

"You had enough already?, caught your limit have you?" he inquired.

I had contemplated trying again, but once he appeared I had gotten so caught up in watching him that I forgot all about it.

"Well, my legs are plum worn out, and these ol' waders have sprung a leak anyways, might as well call it quits" he said.

I nodded in agreement, and we walked back to the car. He was suspiciously quiet. After shedding our wet clothing and heaping it into the back seat, Pinky started the car and turned on the air. We poured hot coffee and sat sipping it in silence as the rain began anew and the wind swayed the great pines overhead.

"Looks like we got out just in time" I began.

He nodded.

I was eager to know how he had done, but knew he would spill the beans in his own good time.

"Saw three raccoons and a possum up by the big boulders" I told him.

He nodded again.

"Only caught one small one, boy they sure were active though' just like you said" I commented.

He swallowed his coffee and nodded.

"How's the log jam above the crick?" I asked hoping to get him to open up.

He looked me straight in the eye for the first time that night and said;

"Next time you do that to me I'm going to tell Cliff the warden how you *really* got that big buck last fall".

He really had been worried. His anger subsided at the end of his sentence. He wasn't one to hold a grudge. It had just caught me off guard.

He then produced a limit of silvery, wet trout from his creel, all fat and glistening, not a one under eighteen inches and relented;

"Now go clean these fish and be quick about it!"

# PINKY

Pinky is my best friend. He could at any given time show up at my doorstep, but his appearance usually coincides with the opening day of trout season in April or some other auspicious event.

From somewhere within his wiry, six-foot frame pours forth insuppressible humor and a child-like interpretation of the world. Only he could sit for relentless hours with his five year-old granddaughter making mud pies, or crawl through the backyard on safari for ants. One day after she had been told that she couldn't keep a stray dog, Pinky caught a praying mantis, and after he persuaded my wife that it wouldn't get loose, he convinced little Ann Marie that it would make a fine pet, better than any dog ever would. She delighted in this and enjoyed catching crickets to feed her new-found pet.

Pinky is always in need of a haircut and shave. His blond curls yield to a weathered, line-creased face. His eyes are as blue as the water of his favorite trout stream and set close together on either side of an aquiline nose.

He amuses himself, when not absorbed in his aircraft sheet-metal business, by luring me into accompanying him on his outdoor adventures, sometimes going to great pains to gain my companionship.

The mere mention of his name has been known to set my wife on edge, doors slamming mysteriously shut in rooms not occupied by myself. His appearance at my house incites an incoherent babbling from her lips that rises in pitch until his departure. Once, the Premonitory Seismic Activity Station called my home just to verify that Pinky's appearance at my house was the demise of their equipment going haywire and not the real thing.

"How bad was it?" I asked.

"Not bad this time....only six point five" came the reply.

"He only wanted to borrow back his waders" I informed them. They should have known, after all it was opening day for cripes sake.....

I first thought that it had something to do with the way that he always showed up with muddy feet right after she had finished washing the kitchen floor, but later rejected that hypothesis when he showed up when the floor was still dirty, producing the same reaction. I finally concluded that it must have something to do with his coincidental appearance, and time for spring cleaning, or some other household chore converging at the same time and space which usually resulted in the chore going undone, and me going off with Pinky.

Most time spent afield with Pinky is memorable. His sharp wit and innate knowledge always ensures a good time. Our caribou hunt is one such time.

We were lazily drifting smelt one April day, trying to entice an early ice-out salmon to bite. The high-back upholstered seats in the boat were very comfortable. My legs were propped up on the gunwale, my back to Pinky.

The morning had been cool and we were layered in heavy clothing. The combination of the warm, noon-sun and the gentle lapping of the waves against the boat caused me to lapse in and out of sleep. Every so often I would open an eye and glance at my pole.

"Ever hunt caribou?" came a question from the stern.

"Whazzat?" I came to a start almost sending my pole to the bottom of the lake.

"Sleeping again, eh? What is it with you nature boys? A little fresh air and you drift off!" Pinky rumbled.

I was embarrassed. The worst thing you could do while participating in any outdoor activity with Pinky was fall asleep.

He asked again "I said, ever hunt caribou?".

"No" I replied.

He knew I hadn't, but it was his way of leading into something bigger. I swiveled around to listen.

"Friend of mine wanted to exchange some work on his plane for a week-long caribou hunt in Alaska, seems he's a little short on cash, said I could bring a friend along…." Pinky said baiting me.

I was all ears. I apologized for falling asleep and promised to return his favorite set of decoys promptly.

"Matter of fact, all the stuff I ever borrowed from you…" I stated.

He put his hand in the air.

"Stop! I'm inviting you…thing is we gotta' think of a way of getting you out of taking your vacation to Hawaii so you can go with me instead" he said.

Good ol' Pinky….always thinking of me.

"Got to be a good excuse or your wife will get suspicious….let's see…hmmm…." Pinky said as he removed his hat, crinkled his brow and scratched his stubbly chin. The omnipresent cigar rolled furiously across his lips.

"I got it!" he barked.

He quickly stood up, violently rocking the boat in the process. I grabbed the side to keep from falling in. Fire flashed from his eyes and smoke billowed from his nostrils.

"I'll call and pretend to be your boss…tell her that we're all backed up at work….that I need you and you'll have to postpone the vacation…." he blurted. He was on fire, and very amused with himself.

I didn't want to undermine his authority, but reminded him that he *was* my boss, and besides, she would know that something was awry if her own father postponed our vacation.

"Why don't we just tell her the truth?" I suggested.

"Boy! You just want to take the fun right outta' everything…don't you!, wives never believe their husbands when it comes to huntin' or fishin', mine never does…" he further stated.

I told him not to fret, that I would work it out-somehow.

"Still think I ought a' call!" he said.

I thought about it all week. It plagued my thoughts throughout each day and haunted me in my sleep. I almost gave it away one restless night when it became particularly bad. I awoke to my wife shaking me.

"You okay?" she said.

"You kept mumbling about… "I'll ask her" or "Alaska" or something….is there something you want to ask me?" she inquired.

"No honey" I said trying to conceal the deer-in-the-headlights look spreading across my face.

I decided right then and there to do it Pinky's way.

When he called I made sure I was unable to answer the phone. I pretended to inspect the plumbing under the kitchen sink.

"Honey, could you get that?…got my hands full here" I said.

She took her apron off, wiped her hands and grabbed the phone.

"Hello?" she said.

"Yes, fine….".

She eyed me suspiciously.

"He's fine…working on the plumbing or something" she answered.

I pretended to be really busy.

"Oh! I see…uh-huh…." she seemed almost excited!

Her gaze went from the counter top to me each time she said "uh-huh".

I feigned indifference and tapped a pipe with my wrench to show I wasn't paying attention and whistled a little tune.

"Really…it's alright" she said.

She turned her back and said something into the receiver I didn't hear.

"No!…really…it's okay" she said again.

"You too…bye!" she said and hung up.

I really-really busied myself.

"That was Dad" she said standing over me with folded arms.

"Oh?…what did he want?" I said coyly.

"Seems he has the chance to go on a hunt in Alaska, and God only knows why, but he wants you to go along" she blurted.

"Really?" I tried not to sound excited.

"When's this?" I asked.

"September" she replied.

"But honey (I really laid it on) that's when we have our vacation in Hawaii!"

"As if you didn't remember that when you planned this last weekend, right?" she said.

I was dumbfounded and it must have shown.

She continued; "It's okay, he told me everything….".

"Everything…?" I asked.

"Right down to how you wanted him to call and make up some excuse to cancel our vacation…I told him you were excused as long as he brought you back in one piece" she lamented.

"Next time try telling me the truth!" she said over her back as she turned to finish drying the dishes.

The next five months practically flew by. It was that last week that lasted an eternity. Pinky and I passed idle time during that frightful week by toning our bodies for the demanding Alaskan wilderness.

This usually consisted of sitting on the couch watching videos of other hunters bagging trophy caribou. By the end of that week we had climbed innumerable ridges, crossed countless streams and trudged miles of tundra. We never believed in doing actual exercise, not when we could watch others doing it and reap the same benefits. Needless to say, we were lean and ready for action. Besides I wanted to present less of an appetizing meal to any hungry Alaskan grizzly bears.. If a bear accosted me I would pinch my arm and say;

"You don't want to eat me, just skin and bones here….". I had read **Alaskan Bear Tales** twenty-seven times and knew just how *not* to become a bear-mauling victim. One piece of advice the book gave was: NEVER RUN FROM A BEAR! That wouldn't be a problem either. With rifle, ammo, hip-waders, three layers of wool clothing and twenty five cans of mosquito spray I wouldn't be able to walk much less run.

Finally the day came. After we kissed our wives goodbye, and boarded the plane, I considered calling my insurance agent to see if my policy covered bear maulings, but then thought, if it covered natural disasters, then surely it must cover bear maulings…besides, what's more of a natural disaster than a bear mauling?

With the aid of a friendly stewardess and a little liquid refreshment, by the time we landed in Fairbanks I had lost all fear of grizzly bears.

Early next morning Pinky and I were waiting excitedly on a small airstrip next to Mike's cabin (our pilot) amongst heaps of gear, comprised mostly of mosquito spray. The day was pleasant for September, slightly overcast.

"Typical for this time of year" Pinky said.

This was his second Alaskan hunt. The leaves had turned their autumn colors and fallen from the trees weeks ago.

"Autumn is barely discernible in the rapid transition from summer to winter at this latitude" he further stated.

Mike arrived slightly late. We exchanged greetings. Pinky and Mike embraced and slapped each other's back affectionately. Not only was Mike a client, but an old Army buddy. They had spent time together in Idaho many years ago. While they talked, I loaded gear into the plane.

Pinky claimed the tiny rear seat. I got in last and sat up front next to Mike.

The engine roared to life. After an unsuccessful attempt to take-off, Mike said;

"We must be too heavy!"

He started to look for things to lighten the load, I snickered and suggested Pinky (only because he had fallen promptly asleep).

Then Mike spied the cases of mosquito spray. With a sideways glance at myself that was a near-miss, but ricocheted off the wall and nearly decapitated Pinky, Mike deposited the cases of mosquito spray on the strip.

Oh well, the next hunters would need them too....

We took off. As we banked tightly, I looked back to tell Pinky how small the houses clinging to the ground looked, but he was still fast asleep. I could barely make out the shape of the mountains off in the east. I believe they were the Alaska Range. Extending from Fairbanks south to Anchorage these granite peaks would be home for the next week. A small ridge called Sheep Ravine was our final destination. Mike knew the location where the greatest concentration of caribou could be found at any time of year. Sheep ravine was a favorite mountain pass used by the caribou to safely traverse the Alaskan Range during their migration to the south each Fall.

Mike's gaze went from the dials and gauges of the cockpit to scanning the horizon and back again. We talked via headsets. I soon learned why Pinky had found a friend in this curly-haired pilot. He was extremely knowledgeable in Alaskan lore, especially all the recent bear maulings.

I found myself looking for a friendly stewardess and some liquid refreshment.

The plane dipped into a small valley and as we climbed on the opposite side, Mike pointed out the tiny airstrip we would land on. It was very short, gravel-covered and pitched upward at a crazy angle. I felt like a Navy pilot looking down at the runway on an aircraft carrier. Our steep descent suggested imminent danger. I looked around. Loud snoring emanated from the back seat and Mike was leisurely gazing out the window. Was I the only one aware of our peril? At precisely the right moment Mike pitched the nose up and applied flaps and rudder simultaneously. The tires crunched down and Mike stood and literally applied the full weight of his wiry frame to the brakes. We skidded to a halt, just shy of the end of the little strip.

The landing had jostled Pinky awake. Yawning, he inquired;

"What?...here already...that Mike, he's quite the pilot, eh son?, you alright?".

Once again Pinky employed one of countless skills and surgically removed my embedded fingernails from the cockpit instrument panel.

"Geez..." he said, "you really had a tight grip on that thing".

I climbed out on the legs of a newborn and promptly urinated, explaining that it might be advantageous to keep the bears from scaring away all the caribou. Mike chuckled in agreement, and busied himself with looking over the plane. I stacked gear in a neat pile on one side of the strip.

Mike reminded us that if we needed any assistance, for a "bear mauling" or anything (he shot a teasing look at me) that we should "place a blue tarp out on the strip". Darn! I had forgotten the blue tarp...I wondered if my cell phone would work out here?

He further stated that he would be flying over the area daily, weather permitting, to keep tabs on us. Then he was gone, the loud whine of the aircraft's engine echoing off the surrounding peaks for a long time after it was no longer visible. I watched our only link to civilization disappear into the low hanging clouds.

If anyone could organize a hunting camp, "even with the burden of a greenhorn such as yourself" he said, Pinky was the man. He was a blur as he shouted orders from his prone position on the soft tundra.

"Don't set the tent there!, it's too damp…no you shouldn't use willow for firewood it will smoke too much!….find some tamarack!" he bellowed.

Before my aching back knew it, camp was tidy and cozy, downright livable.

Pinky surveyed the work.

"Not bad, for a greenhorn…now fetch me some supper!…you know I don't cook!" he said.

After supper Pinky spun tales from previous outdoor experiences. He skipped the bear mauling ones for my benefit. I was drenched in sweat from setting up camp and was looking forward to slipping into dry long johns, when I remembered I had left them at home to make room for the 25 cases of mosquito spray, come to think of it, I hadn't seen a mosquito yet. Oh well, I least I had the nice down sleeping bag. Pinky had crawled into the tent while I tended to the fire. When I finally crawled in myself, Pinky was snoring away, snug as a bug- in my down bag! I didn't have the heart to wake him after the arduous work of bellowing out orders during camp set-up, poor guy, he must have been exhausted. Instead, I unfurled his summer weight bag, which with my toes jammed into the bottom came up to my chin, and settled into a teeth-chattering night. Sleep evaded me. All my senses seemed to be standing guard in the darkness, alert to every rustle and snapping twig. Minutes crept by like lame hours.

Next morning at first light after having finally just drifted off, I was awakened by the clanging of pots and pans outside the tent. My back was stiff. Pinky's nice down bag was empty. I poked my head out the tent flap and was greeted by a steaming cup of coffee. He had a fire going and was actually clean-shaven and smelled of aftershave. He noticed my back was troubling me and said;

"Was gonna' tell you about that big rock on your side of the tent before you set it up, but I figured you would notice…".

"No I didn't" I informed him.

"Not until last night…" I further stated.

"And I couldn't let you sleep in that ratty, old down bag either, so I left you mine, was it comfortable?" he inquired.

"Fine" I said, trying to rub the feeling back into my hands and feet.

"Good" he said, "you can use it the whole week, I won't mind" Pinky said.

He was always looking after my comfort…

Breakfast was fixed by Pinky, consisting of freeze-dried beef jerky which he tossed in my lap.

About the time streaks of orange colored the sky, Pinky declared it time to go hunting. I looked around at the wide open tundra. Occasional smatterings of brush were the only occupants. This was going to be easy! It would be like shooting ducks in a rain-barrel. Caribou couldn't possibly conceal themselves here…they did though', rather well I might add…for the next six days!

Our day consisted of rising at dawn, humping spongy tundra all day, and returning to camp, sometimes after dark. Nights would find me a nervous wreck, listening to all the sounds outside the tent, while Pinky cut chords of wood. I would finally drift off just before it was time to get up again.

After a few days and nights like that, time blurred. I think it was the fourth or fifth day that I was going through the ritual of glassing the surrounding terrain (eyes closed, but I looked like I was glassing), when I spotted a caribou-shaped something about a half mile away.

"Over there, next to that humongous, bull moose…" I said to Pinky. We had only purchased caribou tags because Mike had assured us;

"You won't find any moose in all that wide open tundra…" Perhaps all the caribou were where the moose were supposed to be…

Pinky located the object that I had spotted with his binoculars.

"Nope…only another caribou-shaped bush…you're getting better though'…that one looks like it has a rack on it's head at least" he said.

On the seventh and last day of our hunt we came upon a wrecked aircraft.

Even a hundred air-miles from the nearest human dwelling, it had been picked clean, stripped like a stolen corvette. It lay broken in midsection, with a scraggly tamarack growing through one of the cockpit windows.

"Haven't seen one of these in a long time" Pinky said affectionately.

"What is it?" I queried.

"*It*, is a nineteen-forty-three Aeronica Seldana, can't believe they fitted a sixteen cylinder Franklin engine in her!" he said, admiring the plane.

"See where they added a section onto the nose to allow for room?, she must have eaten some airspace in her days!, will you look at this…!" he started to say.

I had however, turned my attention to the four bush-shaped objects that appeared on the horizon. Even at such a close distance I didn't want to get cocky, so I interrupted Pinky.

"Think I see some more caribou-shaped bushes!" I stated.

"Where this time?" exclaimed Pinky, swiping at a mosquito (which I promptly dispatched with my mosquito spray. Lucky we brought it along, I mean, just think, that *one* mosquito could be carrying all kinds of rare diseases!)

Once his vision was restored from the mosquito spray in his eyes, Pinky quickly assessed the situation and disclosed our course of action. I was so excited I could hardly contain myself!

"You go circle around them and kind a' slowly herd em' this way" he said.

I glassed them again and judged they couldn't be more than a couple hundred yards away and took off smiling.

"See you soon!" I said to Pinky.

Three hours and three rather large ravines I hadn't noticed later, the caribou still appeared to be the same distance away. This tundra is darn deceptive I remember thinking to myself, and launched for another assault. Another two hours later I again stopped. Four sets of footprints all the same size lie in the mud at my feet.

"Amazing!" I thought, four guys been by here, all with the same size feet…thought Pinky said we were alone out here…hmmmm. I glassed for the caribou. They had disappeared. Vanished into thin air. I returned to Pinky. He was laid out on the wreck's wing, puffing on a cigar.

"Darnest thing" I said, "those caribou up and disappeared, and to top it off, we ain't the only hunters 'round here, probably explains why we haven't seen any caribou" I said.

"What makes you say that?" Pinky asked.

"Seen their footprints…" I replied.

"Nah…those your footprints, you been wandering around in circles for over five hours…although on the last pass you got within twenty yards of those caribou….then they got tired of watching you and wandered over here, I nailed a small one…just so our wives will believe we really went hunting" he said.

"Good thinking" I said slumping to the ground exhausted. He pointed to the huge bull caribou which had tree trunk sized antlers.

"No time for rest now, we got to dress out that caribou and get it back to the strip, Mike's due in an hour and you haven't even broke camp yet!" he snorted.

So went our caribou hunt in Alaska, a memorable time had by all. I can't wait for our Alaskan moose hunt. I know a good spot...

# SPRING SUCKERS

It is officially the first day of spring here in the north country. Feels it too. Warm, sunny days followed by crisp, cool nights. Just cold enough to warrant the use of an extra blanket at night.

Folks are busy cleaning up winter's demise. Of course, cold nights and warm days make for great maple syrup. The smell of hardwood fires and boiling sap herald the traditional beginning of the season.

Staring out a northern window at the snow-covered slopes of the neighbor's hill reminds one that winter is slow in releasing it's icy grip. A solitary snow-man, withered and leaning badly, still bearing his red wool cap, stands alone in silent vigil. His melted and re-frozen surface glistens in the midday sun. No need for calendars or clocks, the snow-man's final melting is and has been the benchmark of spring's arrival for years.

The occasional robin, arriving early from his long migration, scampers across sun-melted patches of brown grass and searches for any tasty morsel he might find. Male cardinals call from high atop the row of newly budding maples, challenging all who may enter their territory. Downy woodpeckers also drum, eager to attract a willing mate.

The bird calls subside and the remaining patches of once shaded snow give way to the sun and slowly melt into little rivers that carve out miniature valleys in the remaining snow.

Heat waves rise from the ground as one looks across the hill. The view is distorted with a mirage-like illusion of water coating it's surface.

It is the kind of day where once the shadows lift, one can be comfortable outdoors in a t-shirt.

Alas, melting snow and ice also bring mud, and lots of it. Although mud season is short-lived, it proves to be the demise of many a freshly washed kitchen floor. Rubber boots are the norm here, and best taken off before coming inside.

It is warm enough to open windows again. Spring smells like renewal. It promises hope and clarity after the dreary months of winter. Just a teasing hint of better things to come.

The sky is a hue of blue not observed in other seasons. Cloudless and infinite, it begs the mind to wander...

As a kid, spring was my favorite time of year for many reasons. It meant many things. It meant school was getting close to letting out for the summer. It meant the yearly draining of Millville Lake. But, best of all, it meant the suckers would soon return to the little brook next to our house to spawn.

I had saved all winter, religiously rising early and delivering newspapers before school and on weekends. I now had enough cash to purchase a new fishing pole and tackle just for the blessed event.

Now, suckers are ugly as far as fish are concerned. Not suitable for eating in most folks eyes, they serve no real purpose in life, other than providing pre-summer bass fishing practice for burgeoning, twelve year-old anglers. They feed off the bottom via a gaping hole-of-a-mouth that is tough as the cheaper cuts of steak my mother would buy at the supermarket. They absolutely refused to be caught on any conventional bait, so bare treble hooks with lead sinkers were employed to snag them instead.

It required patience, skill and a little luck, but the reward far outweighed the work. If you snagged one, they gave a tremendous fight.

The key to success was to stand on the cement shelf above the culvert going under the bridge in front of my house. Space was at a premium as all the kids from far and wide would gather here to try their luck. The Hitty Titty Brook was so named years ago by some farmer while observing his cows standing in the brook. The water was just deep enough that a particular piece of their anatomy would barely touch the water's surface. We all knew how it had got it's name because Pinky had told us so.

This spring the water was high and moving fast. The brook's bottom was sandy at the mouth of the culvert, thanks to a little pre-season ploy by us kids. We had removed all the rocks and replaced them with sand. Doing so had increased everybody's chances of snagging the big one.

I don't claim to know the biology associated with suckers, how long they live, what they eat etc., but it was believed by all who fished at this spot that there existed one whopper sucker that returned year after year to spawn. It had always managed to elude being caught. Many school-yard conversations revolved around the big one. Few had actually seen it. Only one kid had the esteemed honor of hooking it. He still goes to counseling and a commemorative spot is held for his pending return to the culvert.

A small crowd of kids was gathered on the shelf, jockeying for position, all the while keeping an eye on the brook's sandy bottom for the tell tale dark shape of a sucker to appear.

"Perhaps it's too early" said one kid.

"Or the water's too fast" said another.

"Nah...they'll be here" said Pinky.

He was the oldest, wisest and second most revered sucker fisherman, first going to Joey, the kid in counseling.

In between conversation about this year's possibilities, kids were busy swapping candy. One rich kid had a whole bag of twizzlers and was trading the less fortunate kids one lousy twizzler for whole bags of less desirable treats. What a racket! Surely he would grow up to be one of those bankers my father always spoke roughly about.

*I* was still stuck inside watching the growing crowd.

"May I pleeez be excused now?" I pleaded over the Saturday breakfast table.

"Finish your juice first…" said my mother.

"But there won't be any spots left on the shelf…" I said through my juice glass.

Finally a knock on the door rescued me.

I started to get up.

"Sit down young man, I'll get the door" said my mother.

She stood up, wiped her mouth with a napkin and walked briskly to the door.

"Well, good morning Mrs. Bingel!" said someone, hiding the toothpick that had been between his lips.

I recognized the voice immediately.

It was Pinky. Good ol' Pinky. He had a knack of showing up during my times of need. If anybody could speed up this process, Pinky was the guy for the job.

"Why, your hair looks absolutely ravishing this morning, have you changed styles?" he buttered her up.

"Thank-you Pritchard" said mother. Only she could call him by the name on his birth certificate.

"I must say, you are up early for a Saturday!" said my mother.

"Why, yes Ma'm, as a matter-of-fact I've been up for several hours now in anticipation of suck…ah…er…sucksessfully appropriating your son for some early morning exercise…" he stammered.

"You mean fishing, right Pritchard?" asked mother.

Uh-oh he was caught.

"Yes Ma'm" replied Pinky.

"Well, we were about finished anyways" she stated.

"Would you like to join us?" she asked.

"No thank-you" said Pinky.

"Your friend Pritchard is here" my mother called to me.

I already had my pole and tackle in anticipation of the outcome.

"Can I go now?" I begged.

"Yes, you can go" she said to our backs as we made haste to the culvert. Pinky had replaced the toothpick between his lips and spoke in short breaths while leading the way.

"That …Mom of…yours…swell lady…don't you…never…tell nobody…my…real…name!" he huffed.

Our toes barely missed the small cement wall as we jumped down onto the shelf. The guys had seen Pinky coming on a dead run and made a hole for he and I. Anybody accompanying him carried the same status and do accord as Pinky himself. I had lucked out…

One poor kid had gotten here late and was banished to fish from the bank in the bushes. It was kinda' sad in a way…we had all had it happen to us over the years. We did offer advice on how to treat the poison sumac he would surely develop in the following couple of days.

The crowd was a buzz of activity, some kids engaged in conversation, others fishing. Another kid was in an overhanging tree keeping vigil for any sign of suckers. From his vantage point, I'm sure he could see plenty of them at any given moment…

Although the shelf was now full, more kids kept lining up against the cement wall awaiting their chance to take a spot should someone leave.

Lines were dangling from poles in anticipation. At least twenty kids were in various locations ready to toss their treble hooks and sinkers into the water at the first sign of a sucker.

Suddenly the kid on the tree limb started babbling.

"b...b...b...b...big one!" he finally blurted out.

We all looked into the culvert.

Now, I have to tell the rest of this story from second hand account, as I don't recall much of what happened next.

Pinky claims that a black shadow the size of a submarine appeared and immediately all twenty kids, myself included, dropped our lines into the water.

"I got him" yelled somebody.

All eyes were on him. But, he had snagged someone else's line, who now yelled also.

"No, I got him!"

Soon everyone was snagged and yelling, including me, or so I thought.

Pinky says that one minute I was sitting next to him, next minute I was yanked from the shelf. He later says;

"It was a good thing that we had removed all the rocks from down there..."

Everyone dropped their poles and did their best to keep up with me as the big sucker dragged me down the brook, yelling that I should let go of the pole.

Later that year while shopping at the mall, I bumped into Joey.

"How's counseling going?" he inquired

"Pretty good...most of the nightmares have stopped" I replied.

Yup, spring carries some great memories for me. And as the day closes and the sky becomes duller and dabbled in pink, the shadows again mount the northern slope, longer this time, meeting the coolness creeping down. The bare, but life-bearing branches of the maples sway gently. The lonely and enchanting song of a towhee, hidden, but visible in mind's eye, brings the day to an end.

Hope I don't dream tonight…

# MELE KALIKIMAKA

As I stepped off the plane clad in my down jacket and carrying my heavily loaded duffel bag, it suddenly dawned on me I wasn't going to enjoy Hawaii. Reading the set of orders that had arrived at my house three weeks earlier, my folks were jealous that a young man of eighteen with his whole life in front of him should be so lucky to get Hawaii as his first assignment.

I on the other hand was suspicious of any place that maintained a year-round temperature of 85 degrees and required sunscreen and god forbid, the wearing of shorts!

I had just graduated from thirteen weeks of Air Force Technical school learning to maintain multi-million dollar aircraft. Boot camp had been made a breeze by having my old buddy Pinky there with me. Having gone to the same base for training afterwards, we spent our last night together and then we both went home for Christmas and to await orders for our first assignments. That was the last I saw of Pinky. I had no idea where he was going or when.

I quickly settled into the Hawaiian way of life and looked forward to a quick two years before I could pick any base that I wanted.

One day I was taking my lunch break and eating manapua, a combination of sweet bread and pork, when some jerk bumped into me and spilled my poi all over my freshly pressed BDU's. I turned to give him a piece of my mind, and who should I be staring at but...good ol' Pinky!

"I thought I recognized that scrawny frame and bad aftershave!" he immediately stated.

"Don't tell me they let the likes of you loose on this island" I retorted.

We both embraced and then quickly recomposed ourselves as we realized other fellow airmen were watching.

"So...Hawaii...huh?" I queried.

"Most god-forbidden place I ever seen!" Pinky snorted.

"Yeah, kinda' how I feel too..." I said.

"No hunting, only saltwater fishing with all that pool-stick sized gear, and way too much sunshine and aloha and mahalo and...." he blurted.

"Look" I said "I gotta' go back to work, but how about we get together this weekend for some fun?" I asked.

"What you got in mind?" Pinky said.

"I don't care, anything, as long as it includes me and you together..." I replied.

"Don't go getting' all sentimental on me now!" he said.

"Sorry..." I replied. "it's just that this place has me all tied up in knots...you know with nothing that really interests me."

"OK, OK...I know what you mean...er...I'll call you tonight!" he said.

And so Hawaii suddenly got a little better after that day. Pinky and I traveled everywhere together. We spent countless hours until the early morning hours at Wahiawa Reservoir fishing for peacock bass and big catfish, almost the same we had as kids back home.

Our two years at Hickam Air Force Base flew by and pretty soon we were ready to part ways again. For our final week together we decided to expand our horizons and plan a week long trip to Kauai, the so-called garden island.

On the night we were to leave a nasty hurricane developed and we had to postpone. The island was hit hard and without power, no planes could land until they cleared the debris. Half the island was being powered by a nuclear submarine. Finally the airlines called and we took a short hop to Kauai. We rented a Toyota Corolla, it was blue and very old and rusted. The interior was a wreck, but it ran and provided home base for five days of adventure, exploring and fishing the many freshwater reservoirs on the island. We didn't have a care in the world.

On our last day after a great day fishing we decided to drive to the North Shore and check out the glider-port. We arrived around 2 p.m. and watched the gliders get towed up and circle lazily around in the prevalent updrafts created by the steep cliffs and ocean breeze here on the North Shore.

Then we had a crazy thought that only first time away from home eighteen year-olds can…let's climb the cliffs and watch the sunset! We quickly assembled our canteens, binoculars and what few snacks we had left.

The first half-mile was easy going, but got progressively steeper. Eventually we were scaling cliffs that were almost vertical. We were both dressed in light clothing, and sweating profusely. The light was fading and going back the way we had come was not an option. So we pressed on and the ground finally became more negotiable. At one point we had to climb a creek bed that ended in an impassable waterfall. It was almost completely dark and I kept running into spider webs. Pinky reminded me all too many times that they were probably black widow spider webs, as much as he could tell with what little light remained.

Pinky called a halt to any further exploration.

"We need to think this thing out, maybe spend the night and try again in the morning" he said, out of breath.

I nodded in agreement.

We took stock of what we had with us. One pair of binoculars. Two empty canteens., and oh yeah…our clothing. How had we gotten into this predicament? Seemed simple enough, climb the hill, watch the sunset, climb down. Oh well, we weren't ones to complain.

Pinky quickly got a fire lit as it had gotten cool. We sat around the dim light of the fire and talked about old times.

"I'll never forget you and those bees…" Pinky started.

Something rolled down the hill from above. Just a loose rock I thought. If Pinky had heard it he didn't let on.

"Yeah, you looked so funny running down that hill…all those bees mad as hell chasing you…I kept yelling…RUN!, RUN! RUN!RUN!….."

"I get it!" I interrupted.

He was looking right at me, or more like through me…

Suddenly he sprang to his feet… "No!, I mean right now…RUN!" he yelled.

Out of the corner of my eye, in the dingy fire light I saw movement.

Bearing down on me was the biggest, and ugliest animal I had ever seen! Now I knew Hawaii had tourist-tame mongooses, brought here to kill all the snakes. I knew Hawaii had black-widow spiders and sharks. I even knew some of the Islands had pigs, left over domestic varieties, but this was no barn-yard pig. This thing had long, razor-sharp tusks and was equal in size to a Volkswagen.

I lurched to my feet and quickly joined Pinky in his quest to escape certain mutilation. He was already scrambling up the nearest tree. I assisted him by shoving from below as I tried to overtake his meager progress. I had the sudden dejavu that we had been here before…

He was laughing so hard that he wasn't getting anywhere. Helluva' time to laugh I thought. The pig charged headlong into the tree, the impact almost shook my grip from Pinky's belt.

"Hey!" he exclaimed "go find your own tree…"

"No thanks, I like *this* one!" I replied.

Then we both started laughing.

Well, we finally got up high enough to escape the marauding pig. Pinky claimed victory and we recomposed ourselves. The only thing left to do was wait until the pig left...

Somewhere around three a.m., long after the fire had died out and the ghastly pig noises had subsided, and the last mosquito had sucked the last ounce of blood from our sleepless bodies, Pinky came up with an idea.

"Why don't you climb down real quiet like and see if that pig has left yet?" he said.

"That's your plan?" I asked, "why me?"

"Cause you run faster..." he replied.

He had a point there. I looked down into the dark void where the ground should be. I could see nothing. I heard nothing.

"I don't know...." I said.

"OK, OK, we'll do it the fair way...scissors, paper, rock" he said.

I thought about the proposal. Even with the dark and clinging to the tree for dear life I knew what the outcome would be.

"I'll do it..." I murmured.

Slowly I inched down the tree, feeling for the ground with outstretched toe.

When I touched down, the ground felt mushier than before------hairier. As my full weight came to bear on the ground, a little light went on in the back of my brain somewhere...you are stepping on the pig... YOU ARE STEPPING ON THE PIG!

"You are stepping on the pig" Pinky squealed or the pig squealed or maybe it was both of them.

"The pig had fallen asleep at the base of the tree, and you stepped on him" said Pinky as I climbed over him on my way to the top of the tree.

No kidding, I thought.

At first light there was no sign of any pig or that anything had happened there at all the night before, except for two very weary Airmen and a few claw marks in a lonely tree on the North Shore of Kauai.

As I said goodbye to Pinky at the airport we promised to meet again in another year or so. I knew it would be a long year.

# HITTY TITTY BROOK

Sometimes in retrospect in our lives we remember what life is really all about. Maybe at any particular moment it entails your first kiss, graduating high school, getting a college degree, getting married, or the birth of a first child. Childhood memories are long forgotten and can surface at odd times. Things you thought were forever gone can suddenly be sparked back to life with the herald of some great happening in your life, or vice versa in the throes of some unforeseen tragedy.

Hitty Titty Brook that ran beside our house where I grew up is emblazoned in my mind. It was the source of many great childhood adventures. It provided a playground for countless outdoor activities. As kids we swam in it. We fished in it. And we even kept it clean and clear of the encroaching brush and weeds that constantly tried to choke it's mere ten foot width. But the best thing I remember about that brook was building rafts and attempting to paddle the distance upstream to the dam at Millville Pond, it's birthplace.

Pinky and I were outside one bright, sunny Saturday morning, up early as usual, sitting on the shelf above the culvert next to my house. We were wrapping paper kitchen matches in tin foil and sticking them in little piles of dirt. These we would light with another match and watch them hurl themselves off the culvert into the water below. We were trying to see who could get one to go the farthest when Pinky got that look in his eye.

He backed into it like he always does.

"You know I was thinking…" he said.

"Yeah, bout' what?" I replied, trying to light a match.

"How many times we been to Mudville?" he asked.

"I don't know…probably three times a week since…like…forever!" was all I could say.

"Yeah, but, ever wonder about the brook and what's between here and there?"

"Not really…OUCH!" I yelled, my match had burned down to my finger.

"Good one, you'll be an astronaut before you know it" he chortled.

"I mean, don't you *want* to know what there is in-between here and there?" he asked.

I could tell he was getting upset so I relented.

"Well, maybe…" I said.

"Never mind…" he said, and started to wrap another match with tin foil.

"No, no…go on, what's your point?" I said.

He ignored me. I had snuffed his idea. I tried a different ploy.

"I heard tell that one kid got lost in the swamp between here and Mudville, word has it that he wandered around all day and night trying to find his way out. After finally getting a break and coming to a clearing he claims to have seen a creature. A creature covered in green slime."

"That story's old, and besides everyone knows Kevin is prone to telling outrageous lies…" Pinky said.

My plan had worked. I played my next card.

"Yeah, but for some months after the creature was discovered, folks started seeing glimpses of him." I paused.

"They even say that he comes out on a full moon and snatches neighborhood cats."

"Malarkey!" said Pinky.

I kept on going.

"Maybe we should go on an expedition, try to see if this creature really does exist." I stated.

"Well…how about this…we build us a raft and just say maybe we do go poking around a little as we explore the brook between here and ol' Mudville…" he said.

We had reached a mutual decision. That was how it was done between kids. His idea and mine melded into one…

We spent the next day building the raft. Mostly we used left over scraps of lumber and whatever we could find for nails lying around my Father's workshop.

That night we slept in my backyard to do a little celebrating. I even brought along my sterno stove and net so we could catch crawdads and cook them up. We planned on supplementing these with fresh vegetables from Mr. Pare's garden, only Mr. Pare didn't know it yet.

After catching a bunch of crawdads we stealthed through a short patch of woods to Mr. Pare's garden. It was about two a.m.. There was a full moon that night. We used no flashlights. His tomato and cucumber crop was ripe and ready for the picking. Pinky and I helped ourselves. As we stuffed our faces with juicy tomatoes, Pinky commented;

"These tomatoes sure are good, only thing is we need some salt…"

Then we tried the cucumbers, again Pinky said;

"These cucumbers are delicious, if only we had some salt…"

At the end of his sentence I felt a stinging sensation in my backside, immediately followed by a loud boom and rather impressive light show. While my brain reeled from pain and tried to sort out the situation, it became apparent that Pinky was afflicted with the same enigma.

Instinctively we both began running to escape the source of our dilemma.

Only then did I see Mr. Pare, clad in nightclothes, pumping that old 12 ga. as he prepared to unleash another world of hurt on us. Luckily, his old piece jammed. He was so mad that all he could blurt out was;

"There's your salt!..."

Fortunately, he had run out of buckshot and supplemented his home made loads with rock salt instead.

Next day, after a uncomfortable night's sleep, we rose early, but never did make the trip to Millville. We hadn't even launched the raft. Actually, my Mother had asked us to clean the mysterious green slime off the porch and search for the cat, it had gone missing since last night...

# Jacques Cousteau and the Vacuum Cleaner

It seems like only yesterday that Pinky, Jerry and I were arguing about the previous night's episode of Jacques Cousteau's Undersea World. None of us could come to agreement with one small detail of the scene with the octopus, you know, where it is wrapped around Jacques' head and trying to pull off his mask...well, Jerry insisted that the regulator looked simple enough to build with a hose from the hardware store and duct tape. But Pinky swore that a similar piece of hose existed in his father's workshop and that it was the same diameter as the one on the pool vacuum.

"As a matter of fact", he sputtered.

"All we have to do...is attach the hose to the pool vacuum, and we have a makeshift air supply!".

He was obviously very proud of himself.

"What about a regulator?" asked Jerry.

"Hmmm...that's simple enough, all we need is a snorkel and some duct tape!" replied Pinky.

Now you know who became engineers later on in life and who still gets paid by the hour...

I just stayed out of the way because in my book I had the most important job of all, "You will be the suck...errrr...the test pilot" exclaimed Pinky.

Anyways, everyone had input on just how to assemble the device. It didn't take long or many rolls of duct tape before we had something that remotely resembled a regulator.

"It will be easy" said Pinky, "all you gotta do is insert the snorkel into your mouth, we duct tape it to your head and then you jump in and breathe in through your mouth and out your nose". Jerry stood beside him and demonstrated like a stewardess on an airliner as he spoke, pretending to breathe in his mouth and out his nose.

On our first attempt without anything hooked up, we discovered that getting me to the bottom of the pool with so much material that wanted to float was going to be an issue.

"No problem..." said Pinky. He produced an old set of lead diving weights that his father had from his Coast Guard search and rescue days and proceeded to place them around my mid section. Each small lead weight attached to the web belt weighed 5 pounds and there were at least ten of them.

"There, that *should* get you down there" he said pointing to the bottom of the pool.

Now we were all set. Jerry was in charge of attaching the hose to the green valve of the pool's vacuum pump which would provide air, the red valve was used for suction.

Jerry stationed himself by the valves and busied himself with attaching the hose. Pinky helped me get to the pool's edge with the added weight. I stood peering down into the depths and was proud, I was like Allen Shepard going to the moon or Charles Yeager test piloting some new jet fighter. Pinky slapped me on the back and gave me the thumbs up. I quickly returned it and he looked at Jerry who also gave a thumbs up. I jumped in and quickly hit the bottom of the twelve foot pool.

"Wow, that was quick" I thought. I had been so focused on the initial experience that I had forgotten to breathe. As I opened my airway to accept that first breath of great engineering, a frightening thought entered my head. It was one of those thoughts that wake you up cold in the middle of the night, not quite sure what has happened, or why you are awake, but very scary all the same. I experienced a minor flashback of glimpsing Jerry attaching the hose to the red valve, the valve used for suction. Then I remembered! Jerry was color blind…he didn't know the difference of red from green. No wonder it had taken him so long. All this ran through my mind in the same instant as my esophagus opened, my lungs expecting to receive life-giving air, but instead had what little was left in them sucked out.

I immediately panicked and swam for the surface, only to realize that I was going nowhere. The extra fifty pounds attached to me were keeping me firmly planted on the bottom. The design had worked flawlessly!

Luckily, Pinky noticed something was awry and jumped in just as I was about to pass out. He hit the quick release on the belt and I quickly jettisoned to the surface.

# GRAVEL-PIT BASS

I was fond of many things as a kid. Mostly doing nothing. But my all time favorite thing that I absolutely couldn't get enough of was fishing. Not just any fishing, but bass fishing. I would tell any lie, pay any amount of money or sell my worldly possessions to spend 1 more hour fishing. Heck, it was more important than life itself to me.

Now, one day while doing nothing and thinking about fishing, I was headed on my bike to the local candy store at the end of the grove from my Grandmother's house. For some insane reason I had quit fishing early to go and get something from the store, Lord only knows why...when I spied an inviting road that I hadn't noticed before on any previous journeys to the store. It was a plain dirt road with only one mailbox, indicating only one residence. I was curious why I had never noticed this road and instead of proceeding to the store I detoured across the tar road and headed down this unknown dirt road.

It was a pleasant road with apple trees lining either side and grass growing up in it's middle. It was unkempt and very mysterious to a twelve year old like myself. Not far down the road and off to the right I spied a gravel-pit. All boys feel a natural attraction to gravel pits, they can't help themselves. It's like finding Christmas presents under your Mother's bed. That's how gravel pits are, little treasures.

So, naturally I stopped and threw my bike down and walked the fifty feet or so to the gravel pit's edge and peered in. There was water! Rain had accumulated and filled the pit to a crystal clear depth of perhaps five or six feet. There were weeds growing in the center, shaped in a ring. And in the center of the weed-ring was the largest bass my eyes had ever seen! I couldn't believe my luck! I almost fell in... I looked around to see if anyone had followed me or was watching me now! All I could think about was catching that bass, it didn't matter how or when, I had to catch that bass.

As I lay on the sandy bank watching her, I just knew it had to be a female, see, females achieve greater body size than males, it had said so in last months edition of Outdoor Life, she slowly finned around her little slice of heaven. A little frog hopped in and proceeded to swim across her weed-ring window. I knew what would happen next. A big swirl and that little frog disappeared! That was enough for me. I grabbed my bike and tore off for my Gram's house. A million thoughts ran through my head on the long bike ride back, what if someone else discovered the bass before I got back? What if Gram wouldn't let me go back? What should I bring for tackle? What if the weather didn't hold? What if they came to fill in the gravel pit before I got back?

Anyhow, I somehow managed to reach Gram's house in just under five minutes and proceeded to grab my fishing pole and tackle box. I was so outta' breath that when Gram asked what was going on I couldn't choke out any words.

"never mind...just be back in time for supper!" she said.

Good ol' Gram, she always understood.

Back at the gravel pit and staring down at the bass I suddenly realized that the walls of the gravel pit were a lot steeper than I remembered from the first visit. The brain tends to miss all those little details when focused on fishing, even at twelve. So, I had a logistical problem to solve.

I certainly couldn't fish from up here. The distance down to the water was perhaps twenty feet. I could hook the bass, but would never be able to pull a fish of that size up and out of that hole.

It left only one answer, I would have to go to the bass. Problem number two, the bass could see me and my approach and swam nervously around the pit creating a shock wave that looked like a small submarine was cruising just under the surface. I backed off. Now what? While I thought I lay on the cool, earthy-smelling sand and watched that bass slowly calm down, until she returned to the weed-ring center and hovered just inches from the bottom. My mind began to devise a plan that would ultimately help me to land that bass. It was pure genius. I even snickered to myself and at the big bass lying at the bottom of that gravel pit.

My plan was simple, remain prone, cast the purple worm attached to my pole in to the middle of the weed-ring and hook the bass. There was no doubt in my mind about that part. She would grab anything that entered her domain. The brilliant part was how I would land her… simple, just jump in and pull her to shore and leave!

A small sign was affixed to a post at one end of the gravel pit. Curiously it had only the number four written on it. The other numbers, three, two and I assume, one, were crossed out…that's dumb I remember thinking.

Anyways, it was by this sign that I decided to launch my attack. The cast was perfect and the worm plopped onto the surface of the gravel pit without hardly a sound and only creating a slight ripple. As I had envisioned in my mind, the bass immediately took notice and began rising to the surface to investigate the source of this intrusion.

I quickly set the hook as the bass engulfed the little purple worm and held on tight. She ran around and around the middle in ever smaller circles shaking her head. When that didn't bring results, she began her aerial assault by launching her massive body out of the water and shaking her head. I somehow managed to keep the line from breaking, falling in or dropping the pole. After what seemed like hours she tired and I decided it was time to bring her home to be admired by Gram.

I jumped down the bank into the water and held the pole above my head.

Reeling her spent body over to me was easy, she was magnificent! Bright green with black lines that ran vertically along her sides. I estimated her weight at seven pounds. Her gaping mouth kept opening and closing as if she was trying to catch her breath from the fight. She seemed to make eye contact with me and question who it was that had finally hauled her from her little slice of heaven. I looked away.

It was then while avoiding her gaze that I noticed that escape from the gravel pit was going to be impossible for me also. Now we were both trapped. I swam to the only flat spot twenty-vertical feet below the little sign and assessed the situation.

A voice above me brought me back.

"Whatcha doing kid?"

I looked up and saw a man in coveralls leaning on the little sign. He was busy scratching something on it with his knife.

"Nothin' I replied.

"Really?" he said, "if I didn't know better, I'd say you were trying to land *my* big bass I put in *my* gravel pit…"

His bass! Did he say *his* bass? Well------I didn't see any signs that said no fishing.

"Nope, and you won't either…, on account these gravel walls are so steep" he stated, and moved away from the sign.

It was then that I could read what he had scratched on the sign. The number four was crossed out and the number five in it's place!

"Five's tried and five's failed…" he said. Then he threw down a rope and told me to unhook the bass and climb up!

Last time I visited that spot, the little sign read nine. Like I said, fishing is my life…

# BANANA SEAT CHOPPER

Do you remember your first bike? Maybe yours was a hand-me-down or bought at a yard sale. One thing remains the same, every kid remembers his first. Mine was store bought from the local K-mart. I got it on my ninth birthday one hot day in July. It was shiny-new, black metal-flake paint with a rectangular, well padded seat and shock absorbers on the front and rear wheels. The knobby tires were designed for off-road adventure. My best friends and I all took clothes pins and attached a playing card to the rear spokes. This produced a clattering noise which replicated a motorcycle engine.

Now, after learning to ride and how the pedal brakes worked, I gained confidence and started doing wheelies and a few small jumps. At one point the town had to fix the asphalt around the little bridge in front of my house. There were storm drains on each side of the walls and they built up the asphalt here to act as dams to prevent drainage into the Hitty-Titty Brook. These little humps made perfect launching pads to practice jumping. The landing was in the grass and softer than asphalt should you wipe out. We rode and jumped here most of that summer, reaching progressively faster speeds. I got quite good at it and believe I held the record for the longest jump that summer. The mark still remains after all these years-five feet seven inches-the total length of my adult body. Of course we eventually grew bored of such a small jump and sought bigger fare. We found it at one of my friend's house down the street. His driveway was roughly ten feet wide and thirty or so feet long from road to the hill which sloped downward at a thirty degree angle.

Someone had come up with the brilliant idea of starting across the street at the neighbor's driveway. That driveway was also the same width and length, and as was the case with developments in that neighborhood, it pitched downward to the street at a steep angle. It was perfect. The rider would start at the top and build speed utilizing gravity and cross the road onto Joey's driveway. We would place a ramp at the end and jump downhill to get maximum height and distance.

Building the ramp was difficult because us kids had so many projects going that not one of us could find any spare plywood in our Father's workshops. Unfortunately, the work-in-progress tree house in my backyard had to sacrifice a wall in order for the plan to reach fruition.

The next morning we all met early at the jump site and quickly prepared the ramp without alerting Joey's Dad to our plan and waited for him to leave for work. Joey's little brother was struggling to move some old snow tires from the garage to the side of the ramp.

A small crowd had gathered around the perimeter of the driveway, spilling out into the street. Word had spread and kids had come to watch. Pinky showed up late and surveyed our work. A few quick calculations using 4th grade math skills and he determined that with the grade of the hill plus pedaling, the rider should achieve a speed in excess of thirty miles per hour. Given the angle of the ramp and the downward sloping hill thereafter, the lucky jumper should travel thirty feet at a height of eight to ten feet off the ground, with plenty of room to stop at the bottom before the backyard ended in trees.

Pinky asked who had the esteemed honor of jumping and a sudden silence replaced the buzzing racket of kids in conversation everywhere…

well-----we hadn't picked anyone yet! We all looked at each other dumbfounded...what an oversight!

Joey's little brother immediately volunteered, but Joey quickly discounted that notion. Joey's bike was in pieces in the garage, and Pinky had walked. Not a rider stepped to the plate to achieve greatness amongst his fellow peers. I looked around. Just when all seemed lost, I heard myself say; "I'll do it...". The crowd clapped and cheered. Pinky slapped my back commenting, "That a boy!".

In that tear-jerking moment I raised my arm and basked in what I felt to be short-lived glory...

I strolled to my bike and proceeded to push it up the neighbor's driveway. Pinky accompanied me while barking orders on what to and not to do. He produced a football helmet and placed it on my head. I gave my bike the once-over, don't know why, but I had seen Eivel Knievel do it prior to his jumps and I wanted to look professional. Oh!, did I mention that I had modified my birthday present only days before? It was now canary yellow. The padded seat replaced by a hard banana seat that was long and skinny. It was cool looking and covered in silver metal-flake vinyl material. The rear of the seat ended in a three foot high chrome-steel sissy bar. The handlebars were a chain welded steering wheel from a 68' mustang in the junk yard that Joey's older brother had wrapped around a telephone pole. Beneath this lay three feet of chrome chopper forks attached to a skinny twelve inch diameter tire. It was beauty, not the best bike for jumping. I worried about the outcome of the jump, but like any nine-year-old-only briefly.

I climbed on and tested the brakes. Pinky gave me the thumbs up as did all the crowd below me. Kids were stacked in an open funnel shape from this side of the road to Joey's driveway along both sides. From my vantage point they looked puny ants. Pinky was grinning from ear to ear and that made me more nervous than anything. I had seen that grin before and it usually always ended badly. I feebly attempted a smile and took off...the chopper performed flawlessly. Even the sudden change from slope to level ground was negotiable once both wheels landed back on the ground. By the time I hit Joey's driveway I think I was well over Pinky's estimate of thirty miles per hour. Kid's faces were a blur in my peripheral vision as I sped by, their voices and whistles hushed by the sound of rushing air in my ears. I aimed for the ramp still pedaling as fast as my little nine-year old legs would allow. The change in grade of the ramp came abruptly, but at such velocity it was smoother than the latter. Traversing the ramp was done faster than you could blink. I pulled back hard on the handlebars to help the chopper get air-born. The ground fell away quickly and I swear I could see the Hitty-Titty Brook over the tree tops. I even had a moment of pre-motorcross creativity and removed my death-grip from the handlebars with my right hand and waved at the crowd while looking over my shoulder. As my attention came to focus on the impending landing I saw Joey's little brother pushing one of those snow tires from the garage directly into my path. It all happened in slow motion. There was no going back. No way to change direction in mid air, or point of impact. This wasn't going to end well...

Somehow the tire rolled underneath the front forks of my chopper and missed my front tire. At the exact moment it was aligned with my bike at a perpendicular angle, we settled right down on it. The tire crumpled and jettisoned both the bike and I into the air. Next time I saw the crowd of kids, they were all upside down.

"That's funny...", I thought.

As I was contemplating the perplexity of this situation, I was again seeing the world right-side up and crunched once on rubber again. I'm sure in retrospect that this happened many times, although I don't recall how many. The bike and I bounced, flipped and became entangled, pieces flying off of the pile like some dragster coming apart during a race. One final landing veered us to the left and into Joey's aluminum sided pool. I went over the handlebars and plopped in. Upon coming up for air some minutes later, I was met with a resounding cheer and clapping. Pinky was first to the crash site and slapped my back with a chuckle and that god-awful grin on his face. I was quickly surrounded by a crowd of kids. My emergence from the pool parted a swath unseen since Moses parted the Red Sea. Everyone wanted to shake my hand.

My chopper was strewn across Joey's backyard, lying in herald to the triumph of my jump. Ah yes, I still remember like it was yesterday, besides, my counselor and I had pretty much played out the Spring sucker thing…

# Josh

Somewhere in every kid's past there existed a dog. A consistent playmate. A constant companion. Never asking for more than attention. To be included. He would walk you to the bus stop on school mornings. Greet you at the door with his favorite yellow tennis ball in his mouth when you returned in the afternoon.

Alas, my father owned beagles. He raised them for hunting rabbits. They were smelly, obnoxious and lived in a kennel outside. Sleep was often fruitless on moonlit nights. They barked relentlessly, at the moon, the neighborhood dogs, and just about anything. Luckily it was short-lived, mostly due to the constant visits from the local sheriff following up on neighborhood complaints. He and my Dad were school friends. They had grown up together. So, eventually the beagles went away. That left the possibility for another household pet. I worked on my Mother first.

At the breakfast table only three days after the last beagle found a home, I tactfully poised the question…

"You know ma', I really miss those beagles…and I been thinking… my friend Pinky's got some really swell Labrador puppies that are just eight weeks old and in need of a good home…".

She was busy cooking bacon, but she listened patiently and intently, so I continued.

"He says they come from good stock and even have AKC registration papers...".

"That's nice dear", she replied.

Well, no denial yet. No affirmative "no!". I had my foot in the door and decided to play my trump card, be direct.

"How 'bout we get one those puppies...?".

I placed my crossed hands under my chin and cocked my head sideways and planted a big smile on my face. It was my best "your little boy loves you" faces I had ever mustered.

She stopped stirring the scrambled eggs and turned her attention upon me. I guess I must have caught her off-guard because at first her look as her eyes met mine was a Mother searching for some good reason why we couldn't have another dog. It was immediately replaced by that softer, motherly look of "I can see this means a lot to you" looks. It was unnerving to have her study me for that length of time, she was literally searching my soul, almost right through me. For a second I almost caved. I quickly regained my composure and resumed the assault...

"I will take care of him, walk him, feed him and clean up after him, pleeeez can I...!!!", I almost begged...the room electric with emotion. I rode the energy. I knew right then she would say yes.

The next day my new black lab friend came home with me for the "trial night" my Father had stipulated when my Mother presented my case in my behalf.

We instantly bonded and became friends. Josh was my constant companion, always at my side. In retrospect I don't know why I allowed the hormonal side of me to become interested in girls. He was all I ever needed. He didn't demand anything of me...yet he commanded my respect and affection. He slept on my bed every night. Eventually after several pairs of my Father's slippers mysteriously disappeared, Josh was banished to a stake and length of rope outside. He never complained and accepted it as a condition of our friendship. Josh was an escape artist rivaling Houdini. He would constantly go missing, only to return hours later. I always wondered what adventures he must have been on during those disappearances...

Over the years and with a little tender prodding Josh came to love outings a-field, whether solo, with me or accompanied by Pinky or some other nameless face. He didn't care, frigid cold mornings with ducks blackening the pink sky or just hanging with the boys on a sunny afternoon after school. At about four years of age, with a wide variety of experience under his belt, I decided that Josh could handle anything. One early April day he proved me right...

It was Spring vacation. One glorious week with no school. Pinky, my assortment of friends and I had run the gamut of things to do. We had ice-fished, hunted rabbits and we were hungry for adventure. It presented itself in the form of the Hitty-Titty brook, our constant source of fun.

Jerry, Pinky and I were at Jerry's house. His backyard, like mine, bordered the little brook. The only difference was one section where the brook flowed into what had once probably been an old field. Some beavers had built a dam and it had flooded. Where the brook flowed in the constant spring flood water had deepened this little pool as we called it, to a depth of three or four feet. Jerry's Dad had dumped loads of sand over the years and created a small beach area here and on hot summer days this is where we cooled off. The fishing was pretty good too. On any day you could catch catfish, eels, bass, pickerel, sunfish, perch and assorted turtles. So, as we stood on this little snow covered beach contemplating our next move, Pinky had a brilliant idea. Since we all loved rafting, why didn't we get as close to the edge of the ice where the brook flowed in and chop a raft made of ice and float around the pool. Sounded simple enough. A point was raised about the integrity of ice in April. However, as Pinky pointed out, the three of us combined couldn't have weighed more than 125 pounds soaking wet (and I hoped the soaking wet part didn't materialize).

"The ice *should be* thick enough and a raft roughly ten foot by ten foot *should be* sufficient to support all of us". Pinky said.

Pinky always did all the hard calculations as he maintained a C average in math, even if it was by having his sister do all his homework and looking over her shoulder for test answers…

We didn't hesitate and made our way onto the ice armed with fresh-cut oak branches. Upon reaching the edge of open water each of us began tapping and chipping away. The ice couldn't have been more than three inches thick here and rubbery. It was slow going chipping away with oak branches. After five minutes I began to sweat and removed my jacket.

What Pinky possessed in math skills, he lacked in organizational skill. Out of the corner of my eye I saw a large crack start where Pinky and Jerry were hammering away. It quickly progressed behind me and as time appears to slow in a dream, I watched the whole section break away and separate from the main body. I was left on a little three by three section. I was close to one side and my weight caused it to sink lifting the other side out of the water. I tried to react, but the slippery ice didn't yield to my already wet rubber boots. I thought about jumping, but the distance was now too great. I did the next best thing-I fell in. I quickly determined that the estimated depth of the pool had been grossly misjudged. I stood four feet seven inches on the bottom and there was at least four feet of water above my head. The current fought to push me downward and under the ice. My wet clothing and boots helped hold me fast to the sandy bottom, but I couldn't fight the current, not to mention the need for some oxygen. I don't recall panicking…just a mild sensation of being in this situation before. Maybe it was the lack of oxygen in my brain or just having been a fisherman all my life, but I swear, down there in the depths of the pool I saw the biggest bass finning slowly on the periphery of the sun-dappled sand. It was dream-like and came towards me. As it came towards me it got larger and larger. I guessed it's total length at three feet. Then I realized it had legs and a tail and an unmistakable dog-shaped head. It was a dog! Josh! He latched on to me and paddled furiously against the current and dragged me to the surface…and air, oh-sweet-air! I gasped and breathed in deeply. Two sets of arms grabbed me and hoisted me up onto the ice.

"We thought you was a goner…!" said Pinky.

"You been under so long that we didn't know what to do…" chimed in Jerry.

"I'm fine" I replied, removing some greenish weeds from my mouth.

"Actually it was quite fun and I wouldn't hesitate to do it again…", I was cut off by Pinky.

"Aw, stop joshing…", began Pinky.

That sentence rang in my head…Josh…where was he?

"Why?, when we left your house he was tethered to his stake", said Jerry.

It didn't make sense. Rather than make myself appear delirious I dropped the subject.

"You okay?" asked Pinky.

On the soggy walk back home I tried to go over the scenario in my head. Maybe I had dreamt the whole thing. They say people experience weird things under stress. In the back of my mind I couldn't wait to get home and check on Josh. I wanted to get there and see him attached to that stake waiting for me, but I knew that meant my dream was due to a lack of oxygen. Still, how did I get out of there? My pace quickened in response. I entered the yard and there he was…securely tethered to the stake. His reaction was the usual tail-wagging and tennis ball in the mouth. I ran over to him and patted his head. I wanted to say so much. I stroked his soaking wet fur…wait…why was he soaking wet! He was securely tethered. He cocked his head to one side and looked me in the eyes. I swear I saw him wink. Maybe he was just reacting to the small greenish weed stuck in his eyelid…

# IF YOU AIN'T GOOD
## YOU GOTTA' BE LUCKY

Growing up as a kid I never played any sports. Mostly I fished. I wasn't particularly good at anything. We occasionally did things that were a trifle dangerous. All kids like fireworks. Procuring them was always the difficult part. In those days they were legal to possess, but you had to be eighteen. Sometimes we would get lucky and one of my friend's older brothers would sell us a handful of m-80's. These we would throw into the culvert in front of my house. They made the loudest KABOOM I had ever heard. A large plume of water would rise up. We never gave much thought to the damage they could do to a hand or finger if they ever went off before throwing them. The next best was the bottle rockets. These we would divvy up amongst teams and have wars. Many of my sweaters bore the scars of past bottle rocket fights, holes burned into them. My Mother would always notice on laundry days.

We also learned that by cutting the top and bottoms off of empty Coke cans and duct taping them together in a cannon fashion that we could use a little lighter fluid and a tennis ball to ramp-up the fun. With enough lighter fluid the makeshift cannons could hurl a tennis ball quite a distance. My upper arms and torso still bear the welts attained during some of those wars…

71

My friend Pinky's Dad worked for the Coast Guard. He did inspections on all the life-rafts and survival equipment. One day we discovered a handful of small silver cylinders in his basement. Further inspection revealed these to be signal flares that were out of date.

"We gotta' try one of these..!!" exclaimed Pinky.

"Looks kind'a dangerous", I retorted.

"Since when you afraid of anything?", said Pinky.

"Besides, we can take them to Mudville Lake and shoot them over the water where there won't be *any* danger involved...", he further explained.

"Looks like they're outdated", I pointed out. "I don't think they'll be any good", I said to Pinky.

"That don't matter, my Dad says they're good beyond the expiration date it's just that they change them once a year whether they need to or not..." Pinky replied.

So, we gathered up the flares and climbed on our bikes and headed to Mudville Lake.

We decided on the dam as our launch pad. It was a short ride through the development and wooded trails. It was early Sunday morning. Had it been any other day or time a crowd of teenagers would be occupying the dam drinking beer they had stolen from their parent's house. Nobody was here. We set up on the cement dam and enjoyed some cans of Mountain Dew and twizzlers that I had brought along. Pinky read the small printed directions on the side of one of the cylinders. After a few minutes we figured out how to make the thing work. The bottom swung open and revealed a firing-pin which was to be used to hit the cartridge by jamming it down on a hard surface while keeping the flare pointed in a "safe" direction.

Because it would be a great honor to actually launch the first flare, Pinky and I had to decide who the lucky candidate would be. He suggested paper-scissors-rock. I had played that game all too many times with him to know how that would come out…so we did it diplomatically. He thought of a number between one and five and I would guess what it was. I was to get three chances and if I didn't get it, he would launch first. Sounded fair to me…

After trying one, three and five Pinky announced he would be the first to launch.

"I was thinking of the number four…" he said.

I should have known, it was the number of fingers he was missing on his right hand.

"Five…four…three…two…one…blast off!" Pinky shouted and thrust the cylinder down onto the cement dam. I had my fingers tucked securely in my ears. Nothing happened.

"Three…two…one…" Pinky counted…trying once more to launch. He slammed the cylinder down again. Nothing happened.

"Here, let me try", I said and reached for the cylinder. Pinky reluctantly handed me the cylinder. As he passed it to me and fortunately it was pointed somewhat towards the lake, it fired. A trail of blazing red phosphorous arched across the lake. Now, let me tell you, the distance across the lake from the dam to the opposite shore was probably a half mile. The little rocket that came from the silver cylinder cleared that distance in just under three seconds. I held my breath. The trajectory indicated that the rocket would make it to the opposite shore. As it entered the tree line a small parachute deployed and the rocket gently floated down into the trees. There were summer cottages there back in those days and it was September. It was unlikely they were occupied.

"That was close…!", said Pinky as he scrambled up from the sand below the wall of the dam. He had taken refuge from the rocket as it left the cylinder unexpectedly during the hand-off.

We whooped and hollered.

"That was spectacular…we gotta' do it again!" Pinky commented.

"Not me…I'm not very good at the launch part" I said.

Pinky's attention was turned to the opposite side of the lake behind me.

"If you ain't good you gotta' be lucky…" said Pinky and his voice trailed off. I turned to follow his gaze. Billows of smoke had started to rise from the trees on the opposite shoreline.

"Lucky that fire doesn't burn down one those summer homes that is…!" he yelled.

Oh no!, I thought. The little rocket had started a fire. We looked at each other and for just a minute we contemplated getting on our bikes and riding home as fast as we could. We didn't, instead we headed for the other side via the tar road that circled the lake. When we got there a small fire had started in the pine needles on the forest floor. This we quickly extinguished and left as soon as it was out. We were pretty sure nobody had noticed.

On the way back to the trail that would take us home, Pinky asked; "You want to do it again?"

"No thanks" I replied. "Not only do I *not* feel lucky right now…I don't feel very *good* either…".

# SLINGSHOT

A ny kid can tell you that one of the funnest and simplest weapons
you can build is the slingshot. They range in simplicity from a
forked branch cut from a tree to the fancier K-Mart variety assembled
out of steel and surgical tubing. Ammunition consisted of ball bearings,
lead split-shot or even the roundest pebbles collected along the banks of
the Hitty-Titty Brook.

Finding targets was easy. Empty soda cans filled with stones and
hung from a bush provided hours of entertainment.

One day Richie Brown came pedaling up to the culvert. Pinky and
I were assembling nut and bolt bombs. Richie was sporting a brand
new bike from his birthday last weekend. He had begged his Mother a
million times and she finally gave in. Richie had the fastest, biggest and
newest of everything. He was separated by many years from his older
brother and the only child still living in the house. His parents gave him
anything he bugged them about long enough for.

Richie had the ever present red licorice hanging from his mouth
as he put the kickstand down on his bike and joined Pinky and I on
the shelf over the culvert. His curly red hair stuck out from his ball cap
accentuating his round, freckled face and brown eyes. He had been born
an overweight baby and was destined to go over 250 by his senior year

in high school. Although no one had ever seen him mad, it was thought best to stay on his good side and retain his friendship.

"Making nut and bolt bombs?" he asked.

"Yep…" said Pinky.

"Can I help?"

Now, making nut and bolt bombs is a delicate operation, an art if you will. It required skill, patience and focus. Three things that Richie had little of.

"Actually, we're almost finished" I interrupted.

I began picking up the remaining pieces and stuffing them in my pockets.

"Can I have just one…pleeeez!" Richie begged.

He picked one up and placed it in his jeans.

Well, couldn't say no to that.

The assembled ones Pinky and I wrapped individually in bubble wrap and placed gingerly in a Ked's sneaker box.

We indulged Richie, mainly to pacify him, we had no intention of letting him use any of them, minus the one now in his jeans.

"I'll let you try my new slingshot…" he said and produced a sleek, black slingshot from K-Mart.

Pinky and I had graduated from tree limbs to models cut from laminated plywood. We were proud of them and they served the purpose. These we always carried in our back pockets. But this thing was beautiful.

I could feel my hand reaching for it before my mouth even produced any words. All boys have an affliction for works of art in the form of a weapon.

Pinky watched in disgust as I grabbed the slingshot from Richie's hand.

"Here's some ball bearings" said Richie.

I palmed a handful of the cold-steel beauties and placed one in the real leather pouch. I admired the quarter inch surgical tubing and molded hand grip. There was a wrist brace integrally built into the handle for stability.

I pulled back as far as I could and took aim at a lily pad in the water below. The sound that ball bearing made as it hit the water reminded me of a scene from Bridge over the River Kwai where the Japanese are shooting at the American GI's underwater. I could almost picture the little ball bearing embedding itself in the sandy bottom of the brook.

"Wow…!" was all I could muster.

"Ain't it great!" exclaimed Richie.

"Ain't it great…" said Pinky under his breath.

He took out his slingshot and grabbed a pebble from his jeans. He pulled back on that sun-bleached canvas pouch, cut from some sneakers and those old rubber bands. Just before releasing the bands broke and smacked him on the hand.

"Ouch…darn…!" yelled Pinky.

Richie snickered a little and offered the new slingshot to Pinky. He reluctantly took it. He eyed it suspiciously. Suspicion turned to curiosity and then admiration as he pulled back on that surgical tubing. After shooting it a few hundred times his opinion changed.

"Hey! I got an idea…let's hide in the bushes and shoot passing cars…" said Richie.

Just for a moment I could picture a ball bearing passing through the hood and into the engine block of some poor guy's new Oldsmobile. I quickly erased that thought.

We've all had bad ideas and made poor choices in our lives, but somehow this one seemed like fun…I quickly replied, "Let's do it!".

It was late spring and the Hitty-Titty Brook was swollen with ice melt. Normally dry places were flooded. We chose some bushes and hid, until Pinky pointed out that they were poison sumac and we had to move. I made a mental note of the last known location of our household bottle of calamine lotion. We found a suitable spot across from my house and gathered in a small semi-circle of alders on the edge of the flood water. It was now dusk and the street lights glowed fluorescent yellow in the twilight. Few cars pass through this neighborhood after dark. We waited. We swatted at mosquitoes. At one point I stopped Richie short of releasing a world of hurt on the family cat and shooed it away.

Richie shared licorice as a sign of good will and no hard feelings. He even placed the new slingshot in my hands and said; "Here, you get the first shot…".

It was an honor.

Headlights shone on the bushes and the roar of a V8 announced the arrival of our first victim. My heart raced and sweat beaded on my forehead.

I couldn't get a ball bearing into the leather pouch I was so exhilarated. Richie saved the day and fired mine with ammunition he produced from his jeans pocket. I caught a glimpse of a bolt shaped object in the streetlight as it left the slingshot and impacted the back window of the car. It shattered, followed by a loud BOOM!

We couldn't contain ourselves and broke out in laughter.

The occupant jammed on his brakes, followed by the driver's door opening up. The pair of cowboy boots that stepped onto the asphalt were unmistakeable…

"Oh no!" said Richie.

It was his older brother, Mark. Mark was furious. He quickly assessed the damage and kicked the rear tire several times. Explicatives flew from his lips like so many doves escaping a magician's hat. He looked around and spied Richie's bike still kick-standing next to the culvert.

"RICHEEEEE….!!!" he hollered.

We all took off running with Mark in hot pursuit. Richie quickly fell behind. His brother had not been genetically predisposed to the family DNA. He was tall, skinny and athletic. He had played football in high school, running back I think. The only thing in our favor was fear and an extensive knowledge of the backyards we traversed in our flight. Mark knew nothing of the welded wire fence surrounding Mr. Pare's garden, which gave us a sufficient lead when he tripped over it. We were running out of dry land and I leapt to a pine branch and quickly shimmied up with Pinky right behind me. Richie was unable to make the jump and waded the brook until he was hidden behind some flooded bushes.

It was deafly quiet. We dared not whisper a word. Minutes crept by. Faintly I heard splashing which grew closer. The splashing stopped and a flashlight beam appeared below the pine. In it's glow was Richie and my lab Josh with his front paw in the air pointing at him.

"Good boy!" said a voice.

It was my Father. Mark had gone to my house and enlisted his help.

"You alone son?" queried my Father.

Now all kids have an unwritten code of honor. We don't squeal on each other.

"Uh, yeah..." replied Richie.

"It was just me...all my idea" he further volunteered, selling the story.

"You're gonna pay for my window!" Mark stammered.

"I know, I know..." said Richie, "Just don't tell Ma'...pleeeez" Richie begged.

"Let's go home, get your bike and put it in my trunk" Mark said.

"Thanks for your help Mr. Bingel". He shook my Father's hand and grabbed Richie by the scruff of his neck.

"Watch the poison sumac, it's everywhere around here..." said my Father, shaking Mark's hand.

They all left and Pinky and I exited the tree.

Nothing was said when I got home later that night. However, when I went to my room a bottle of calamine lotion was on my pillow with a small hand written note that said;

"Some lessons are not learned until later on in life, for you that should surface around tomorrow morning".

The next morning while applying lotion to my itchy arms and face I reflected on that advice and the point was well taken…

# THE SUMMER COTTAGE

I recall it like it was yesterday, from the moment my two sisters and I stepped out of Mom's 67' Chevy wagon. The drive had been long and hot. My sisters and I had fought most of the way. The driveway was dirt and overgrown with grass. The sides were lined with wild blackberries and white birch trees. The cottage my grandparents had purchased as a summer place on Country pond was small. It was aqua, my grandmother's favorite color. Pop had just finished painting it recently. My parents headed for the porch steps and I for the water.

There was a small wooden dock jutting out into the water. It was old and rickety and with reckless abandon I ran it's full length of 20 or so feet and admired my new playground. The pond was sparsely populated with a few other cottages.

Peering into the blackish water I could not see the bottom, although it couldn't be more than a few feet deep. To the right there was a large patch of lily pads and an inviting tree stump that stuck up from the water's surface. I just knew there were bass here and those lily pads had to be the first place I would hurl my rubber purple worms into. I could hardly wait!

My mother called to me through the front porch door...

"Steve...come say hi to your Nana and Pop...!"

I obliged and reluctantly left the dock to be hugged and kissed by my waiting grandparents. My gram wore a flowery blouse and aqua polyester slacks. She smelled of cigarette smoke and too much perfume. She wore black glasses. The magnification of the lenses yielded to her steel-gray eyes. The whites contained little streaks of red blood vessels. My eight year old mind could not fathom the reason for this phenomenon.

She hugged me all-too-tight and left lipstick impressions on my cheek. My Pop hugged me also. His stubbly face was scratchy and he smelled of pipe smoke and Old Spice aftershave. His kisses were always wet and required a swipe with the back of my hand on my cheek. His eyes also set inside glasses and that same blood-shot redness evident. His hair was salt and pepper, cut in a crew cut popular for that time.

My grandparents were frugal. They had scrimped and saved for the luxury of buying a summer home. Gram was retired and Pop still worked at the shoe factory. What or where it existed I knew not. He often came home smelling of machinery and oil. So I fabricated in my mind that he must be a maintenance guy. Toiling in a shoe factory and keeping the stitching machines functional. I never confirmed this.

Their real house was a very nice three story 5 bedroom, 3 bathroom house on Main Street in Plaistow, N.H.. It was just down the street from the barber shop where I got my haircut on Saturdays after going to the dump with my father. Joe, the proprietor, I assumed was an old friend of my Dad's. His shop was a buzz with customers reading assorted Outdoor Life and Field and Stream magazines. The radio was always playing. It was always smoky and Joe always placed a plastic wrapped lollipop in my hands after he cut my hair. I decided I liked him from the first time I met him. He always spoke of flying his float plane and how he someday would open a campground. As far as I know he did...right on Country Pond, just down the shore from the Boy Scout camping area.

Almost in unison they both asked how old I was now and commented how big I had gotten. My focus remained on that dock and those lily pads.

After my parents had forced me to sit and chat for awhile Gram went to the cabinets above the sink and produced a Maxwell House coffee tin and removed the lid. I was busy playing with my collection of hot wheels. I had just celebrated a birthday and one of my best friends had given me a plastic case to store them. I was busy sorting and admiring my collection.

She held it out for me to remove one of the multi-colored tootsie pops inside. I loved these and picked grape. The wrapping had numerous pictures of cowboys, astronauts and the like. My favorite were the ones that had an Indian on it...my sisters and I consider them to be lucky. I scoured all 4 square inches of it...no Indian today.

Rumbling thunder could be heard in the distance as my folks hugged me goodbye and ran to the car with my two sisters in the pouring rain. Great I thought, alone at last and it's gonna' pour. My Gram, Pop and I sat on the porch and watched the rain pound the pond's surface until it got dark. Bats flashed in and out of the feeble light that extended beyond the boundaries of the porch. An occasional moth brushed it's wings against the screens.

We played board games on the small wooden table on the porch, the flickering candlelight casting shadows on the knotty-pine of the cottage walls. I found that by staring at the black knots and using a little imagination they started to materialize into faces. There was one that looked like a witch's face. Another that resembled an old man. Even one that looked like my sister in the morning with a big yawn spreading across her mouth.

Sleep alluded me that first night on the couch pull-out bed. It was Monday morning and Pop was up early. The coffee percolating and the smell of eggs cooking was a pleasant awakening. I could hear him in the bathroom with his electric razor shaving. I drift in and out of laziness and when I awake for real Pop has left. I quickly throw on clothes and grab my fishing pole and head for the dock. The sun has not yet made an appearance. Robins are just starting to stir and practice their morning voices.

I creep out to the end of the dock and cast my purple worm towards the lily pads before I stop walking. It lands with a loud plop. I watch the line as it slowly sinks. Suddenly the line jumps and begins slinking out. Something has swallowed the worm and is heading away. I wait patiently and turn the reel handle until it clicks shut. When all the slack line is gone and whatever on the other end starts pulling I set the hook and start reeling. My rod is about four feet long and the reel is a Zebco 303, it was better designed for handling small perch and sunfish. The largemouth bass that I have hooked jumps out of the water and my eyes widen when I see how big it is. I hold on for dear life and struggle to tighten the drag as the bass strips line from the reel with a loud ZZZZZZZZZZ....noise. I whoop and holler. After a couple minutes I get the fish dragged to shore by walking backwards down the dock.

I quickly unhook the monster and let it go. Wow! I can't wait to cast again. The second cast is uneventful until I get the purple worm all the way back to the dock. The sun is now penetrating the water and in a sunny spot as I look down, ready to lift it out for the next cast, a huge bass comes from under the dock and engulfs my worm and immediately starts to swim off. There is no slack in the line and I scramble to push the bail and let him take it away where I know he will eventually get the hook in his mouth. I almost blow it and feeling the pressure he spits it out. Oh no…! I recompose, unbelieving that he is still there eyeing the worm suspiciously. I only have to move it once and again in the blink of an eye he opens that gaping mouth and inhales the purple worm. This time it is all the way in and I set the hook…then hold on. The drag screams as he heads for deeper water. This fish chooses not to jump and we stay locked in battle. The little rod bends to it's breaking point, but somehow does not. One of the eyes on the rod comes out and still he is on. I swear, I fought him for a half hour. I realize I am not going to land him the same way as the first and start hollering at Gram to bring a net to help. She appears at the cottage door, her hair awry, horn-rimmed glasses missing from her sleepy face.

I yell for her to bring the net. Finally she realizes my dilemma and rummages through the wooden box where it is stored. Still in pajamas she comes to my rescue and scoops up the prize.

I called my Dad and recounted the whole story. He couldn't wait to see it. Gram and I hung it on a length of rope off the end of the dock. I wanted it alive so as to release it afterwards.

When my Dad came that night we went to the end of the dock. I pulled the rope up and all that remained of that bass was it's big head, the rest of it-gone! We later determined that a snapping turtle had come and eaten that fish alive.

Only a single, worn Polaroid exists of that bass. He weighed four and a half pounds. My largest to date at that age. In the photograph I am skinny. My red hair is crew cut. There are freckles on my tanned face. I recall I could barely hold the fish while Gram took it.

The rest of the week found me exploring the tar road which continued beyond my grandparents house. The trees hung over from both sides and formed a tunnel effect as I strolled that was mysterious and added to the aura of this new place. The road passed a few cottages and a few houses that appeared to be more than mere summer homes. The road curved sharply right and ended abruptly at a spot that narrowed into a point. The sides dropped off steeply to a wisp of shoreline. The trees here were huge hemlocks and the ground was littered with needles. It was dark and cool, very little sunlight filtering from above.

A small island was visible from here. It was a stone's throw across a shallow cut. Many old cabins were visible just inside the tree-line, begging to be explored. I needed a boat.

Gram had an old aluminum rowboat that I remember seeing pulled up and stashed in the bushes to the side of the dock, perhaps she would let me use it?

So the size of my playground increased…once I proved my swimming skills and after receiving a life preserver and instructions from Pop that evening when he returned from work, I began to plan my attack for the next day.

I barely managed to eat or sleep that night. Today I find it hard to rise at the same hour that I did in those days. I was up well before daylight, just after Pop left for work. I faithfully placed the life preserver on and threw my tackle box and rod in the rowboat. I shoved off and once I got the oars fixed in place, headed out. I immediately headed towards the island, but then thought that I had all day and should go left from the cottage and tour the pond in it's entirety.

Only a short distance from Gram's place and I was at the culvert and bridge that provided access to Wilder's Grove. I sized the culvert up and realized that the little rowboat would fit through. Inside the culvert it was dark and noisy. Every clang of the aluminum rowboat amplified by it's walls. The depth was shallow and using a single oar I could push off the bottom and guide the boat through to the other side. Once I was out it was evident that the passage led to another secret smaller pond. I could see it's mirror like surface only fifty feet away.

The secret pond had no houses around it. It had no real shoreline. The brush had grown right to the edge of the water. Evidence of beavers was everywhere. They had made passages that led into the brush. It was very inviting and hard to stayed focused and not just follow one of the numerous resulting streams back into the brush.

Across the two hundred foot width was a small wooden dock, badly worn and obviously not used for many years. It was actually just the footings and a few planks that remained of what used to be a dock. It was here that I chose to stop and fish.

I could barely contain myself and the good fortune of choosing to come this direction first. A kingfisher fluttered from one of the dock pilings and chastised me for disturbing his rest. Dragonflies floated by and occasionally one lit on my rod tip.

My first cast was met at the surface with a bath-tub sized swirl and my monofilament line jerked and all the ensuing curls on the surface went taught.

I caught so many bass that morning…as a kid you never really keep track. The only reason I left that secret pond was to head back for lunch. Besides, it would always be here and I could come back whenever I wanted.

Lunch at Gram's always consisted of a big, crystal pitcher filled with Carnation instant milk and we ate Hollywood bread stuffed with liverwurst and yellow mustard. Gram made cakes as a sideline and always kept the trimmings for me. These I relished, especially the crunchier bits and pieces.

I never did make it to the island that day.

# COMBAT FISHING

I swatted at the swarm of mosquitoes floating around my face and gazed upstream. It was impossible to tell what time it was by the color of the dappled light filtering through the overhead birches. I guessed 10 p.m. but looking at my watch I was surprised to find it was 4. Wait, 4 p.m.? I had started fishing on Friday night at 7 p.m. after finishing work, driving home and piling gear into my truck and making the one and a half hour trip to the river. What day was it? I felt like I had only been here a couple hours...I asked the closest person next to me what day it was.

"ya, combat fishing has a way of doing that to you...it's Sunday..." he replied.

Combat fishing. Fishing the one river in interior Alaska that flows from the south to the north, standing three feet away from the next person, in a long line of fisherman. All of us sharing a small gravel bar where the Salcha River is met by a nameless glacial runoff stream. It is where the King salmon return in July to spawn. It takes them all summer to get here. They are weary, but once they meet the cold, clear runoff of their birthplace, they become invigorated. They sit in deep holes, resting from the long journey until they move upstream to continue the circle of life. There are also rainbow trout here. And they too are spawning. The Kings greedily eat the eggs that become dislodged and renew their strength for the final push upstream. It is my hope that the netted bag of salmon eggs will entice one into biting and provide me with a fish---one that won't fit into my double-sink---36 plus inches long and weighing 40 or so pounds.

Pinky had come along to keep me from getting lost and so I could help him carry out his catch. Our trip had been uneventful until we were half-way to the river. I looked ahead on the wooded trail and noticed a rather large grizzly bear meandering in our direction. It saw us and luckily headed into the woods before I could tell Pinky. Pinky disliked bears. However, they seemed to be attracted to him. Probably because his mind was continually "fishing"...he lived and breathed fishing. When he wasn't fishing, he was talking about fishing. When he wasn't talking about fishing (because he couldn't *be* fishing)...he was thinking about fishing. All that karma must give off an invisible scent that we humans can't detect...

I thanked the fisherman for the time and looked for my friend Pinky amongst all the other red wool shirts lining the gravel bar. There he was! He had managed to secure prime real estate at the confluence of the glacial stream. The fishing was best there. He was busy holding his rod up high and allowing the salmon eggs to bounce along the rocky bottom. I could see his rod tip move slightly as the bait moved along. Suddenly the guy next to him hollered "fish on!". His rod bent as he struggled with setting the hook. Pinky and the person to the other side of him yielded to his movements. Only a few feet separated each from the other, but that's how it was. If you had one on everyone reeled in and watched, but did not risk losing their spot.

A rather large hooked-jaw king salmon jumped from the water thirty feet away from the guy. A red bag of salmon eggs was visible and securely fastened in the corner of it's mouth. The guy's drag hummed and eventually after a tedious battle the fish was dragged onto the bar. By this time everyone had resumed fishing.

Pinky threw his line in and immediately he was also hooked into a fish.

"Fish on!" he bellowed. Smoke from his cigar plumed up from his lips. I started in his direction to help. I was looking down to prevent slipping on the algae covered gravel and when I looked back up I noticed everyone around Pinky was slowly backing up. Pinky had the same effect on me when engaged in fishing. I could watch him for hours. Then I also noticed the same blonde grizzly I had seen two days earlier on the path sauntering along the gravel bar. Fishermen began scattering in all directions.

Pinky called to me "...come here my boy, I need your help!" "you see the size of this pig!" "he's a real bear!".

No, I immediately thought, the real bear is just behind you...

Pinky kept up the battle. "here son!" "come here...I'm gonna lose him!"

He was losing patience and shot a look in my direction. I think it was the fact that usually he would have seen 20 other fisherman between he and I that made him suspicious, but I believe it was the sheer look of terror on my face that caught his attention first.

His gaze followed mine as he swiveled around. The grizzly was now less than 15 feet away from Pinky. It's massive head was swaying from side to side as it tried to decide who was intruding on it's favorite fishing spot. Right at that moment it stopped and stood up on it's hind legs. It towered over Pinky.

I was unable to speak. Surely it was the last time I would see my friend alive...

Now, I told you Pinky doesn't like bears, but I didn't say he was afraid of them. He yelled at that old bear----"go find your own spot to fish!"---maybe out of lack of anything else to say, but there wasn't any fear in his tone. They gazed at each other for a split second...I thought I

90

saw Pinky wink at that bear, anyways, the grizzly dropped back down. Then Pinky turned his back to the bear and continued to fight the big king. The grizzly turned and headed back towards the woods…honest to god! There's no messing with Pinky when he is focused.

I never did catch my double-sink fish that trip, but on the way out later that night while carrying one of Pinky's salmon, he fell behind. I figured he was tired. I swear I saw him dropping one of those prize salmon on the trail. He quickly caught up and explained that he had to "fix his waders…they were rubbing the corn on his big toe".

I looked back in the direction he had come and thought I caught a glimpse of a blonde bear picking up a rather large salmon in it's mouth. It hesitated but a moment and looked in our direction. Maybe I dreamed the whole thing, after all I had been up for almost 72 hours…

# GETTING LOST FOR DUMMIES

No one who spends a fair amount of time in the woods would tell you otherwise. Nothing is worse than getting lost. It isn't just the plague of green-horns. It can happen to the seasoned woodsman.

I had perfected the art. Starting with boy scouts and learning map and compass skills. Mr. Blodgett worked at the local hardware store by day. On Wednesday nights he taught the local scout pack the art of orienteering. Unfortunately, I spent more time goofing off in the pumpkin patch with two other boys. I think I missed the whole seminar.

It progressed to college during many walks in the woods plotting logging roads and map and compass to navigate woodlot to woodlot for timber management. I was engrossed in birds, fungus, just about anything other than navigation skills.

My Dad started taking me hunting at a young age. By age 8 I had my own .410 bolt-action shotgun and would accompany him and my uncle to deer camp. I always stayed close and never wondered how they found their way around the big woods of northern New Hampshire. They just did. Radios were standard procedure, although they were cumbersome in those days. They allowed my dad and uncle to check in with each other. They discussed where they would meet for lunch mostly. Occasionally, my uncle would shoot a deer. I think my dad never did because he was toting a non-stop-question-asking boy.

As I grew older my dad would bring me to an huge oak tree next to an old farm house stone foundation. We had sat there many times before. He even had mice that would come and take bits of crackers from his hand while on stand. I was left alone and told he would return at dark to get me. I enjoyed that long hour or two alone. I would raise my gun at big-antlered bucks and pretend to squeeze off a shot.

Then one day while in unfamiliar woods, my dad and uncle gave me a radio and I was instructed to walk away from the sun ½ mile where I would join the logging road and wait until they met me. I was no longer a rookie, but a partner in the firm. I beamed from ear to ear. I checked my gun, safety on, radio on, and headed off with the sun at my back. I was focused. I took three cautious steps, stopped and looked around. I did this for the first ½ hour. After no deer popped into view I lost interest.

I also lost track of where I was and what direction I was headed. Pretty soon I was totally turned around. I could not remember which way I had come from. The sun was now obscured by clouds and it was getting dark. I tried the radio. I could hear my father and uncle talking. They were asking each other if either had seen me. Then I lost them altogether. Being young and inexperienced I felt no panic...no sense of urgency to get anywhere. I looked around and picked a new direction hoping that I would hit the logging road soon. The terrain changed and became steeper and steeper. Soon I was grasping small trees and pulling myself upward. The canopy above my head closed in and it got really dark. I crossed a small stone wall and it gave me assurance that I was near civilization. It was a false sense as it was an old stone wall that had perhaps been there since the Civil War days.

It became too dark to safely travel without the help of my flashlight so I stopped and procured it from the small fanny pack around my waist. The batteries in the radio were almost dead so I placed it into the pack and headed uphill once more. Once I reached the top perhaps I could see where I was. I must have walked for a couple hours. I was drenched in sweat and getting a little worried. Certainly my father and uncle would be looking for me by now as I was overdue. Looking upward I could see an opening ahead and continued on. The ground no longer was dirt but solid ledge. The trees became fewer and were scraggly and small. I broke out and saw a fire tower only a hundred yards ahead! I was *somewhere*! I quickly made it to the tower and looked around 360 degrees. Although it was dark I could see the terrain, even a smallish pond down in the valley. There were no lights…no houses…no roads. My hope slumped and I think it was at that moment that I gave in to fear and panic. I quickly tried the almost dead radio. No luck. I immediately started down the mountain totally unaware where I was headed. I think I went down in the opposite direction from which I had come. I semi trotted and ran blindly down that slope, occasionally stumbling and falling. Luckily I did not hurt myself.

When the ground became flat once again I was in a swamp and had to skirt it's edges. I had no sense of time and my flashlight was dying. I became afraid I would run into a bear. I stopped and listened to the silence. I then decided to fire my shotgun in three evenly spaced shots. I hated to waste the shells but remembered from hunter safety class that it was the universal call for help. The blasts rang out loud and echoed off the surrounding hills. Then it was deafly quiet once more. I guess I expected that someone would return fire or at least yell asking if I needed help…only silence yielded as the last echo ended. I hung my head and piled up on the ground. I wanted to cry. I was all alone. My mind was getting the best of me.

I wanted to start a fire, stay put and wait until morning to continue. I was afraid of spending the night alone in the woods. Would a bear get me…? The fear got my adrenaline flowing again and I started off in yet another direction. I went slower this time. My flashlight died as I came upon what appeared to be a very faint logging road. It had not seen human use in a long time, but it rejuvenated my spirits. I looked in both directions. Which way to go...? It appeared that logs had been dragged in one direction versus the other. Had they been dragged out of the woods or cleared inward as the logging operation was progressing...? No time for indecision. I chose left and took off walking. If the trail dried up I would turn around and head the other way. At least I was on a human made trail! Within an hour the faint road became a well used road. It was muddy and tire tracks became evident. Ahead the road twisted sharp right. From around this bend came headlights. A white van appeared. My mind was thinking deer hunters leaving the woods late. Little did I realize it was 3 a.m. and I had been walking for almost 11 hours.

The van pulled up and a friendly, elderly gentleman popped his head out the window.

"You must be Steve..." he said.

I stared at him in disbelief and relief. I wondered how he knew my name.

"There's a lot of people looking for you" he further stated.

"You are about 23 miles from where you should be" he then told me.

I asked him if he could give me a ride.

"It would be my pleasure..." was the answer.

My father was happy to see me. So were the two New Hampshire game wardens, four New Hampshire state troopers and assorted hunters and volunteers who had been looking for me...

"Let's not tell your mother about this..." were there first words out of my father's mouth during that reunion.

# KANGAMANGUS HIGHWAY

My parents both worked when I was a small boy. We could not afford elaborate vacations over the summer. Once school let out I was left home alone or at my grandmother's cottage for most of the summer. I managed to keep myself busy.

I always looked forward to camping with my family. My father would get out of work on Friday and rummage around in the garage for all of our camping gear. The family station wagon would get stuffed to the gills with tent, sleeping bags and the like. My father had built a wooden cabinet that held all of the various cooking utensils and food. It was very ornate with brass hardware and even had a towel rack mounted on one of the doors that swung open. I was allowed to bring my bike and fishing gear.

We visited many campgrounds over the years. Gunstock was a large ski area that also was utilized for camping. It had an outdoor swimming pool, a store that sold night crawlers and a pond that held silvery, stocked, rainbow trout.

I could hardly contain myself the whole drive there. Then there was the unpacking…setting up the tent, driving to the campground woodshed and loading and unloading firewood. Somehow I looked at all this as cutting into my fishing time and as hard work. My father's quiet demeanor would melt away into relaxation and he even talked to me. He and my mom became friends again and hugged one another. I think they even kissed.

I remember the chipmunks being rather prolific. They scurried about the campsite. My mother even allowed us to lie down with a peanut in our lips and eventually the chipmunks would crawl onto us and grab the peanut. In retrospect it was probably the most "dangerous" thing she ever allowed us to do. My two sisters would go on many walks. I suspect to check out the local boy population.

My dad spent most of his time in a lawn chair drinking a cold beer and reading or just relaxing.

I on the other hand was always on the go. I made many friends over the years and they often returned to the same campsites. It did not take long before we found one another and headed out for some adventure.

One morning I got up early before anyone else and climbed to the top of the mountain. There was a maintenance trail and it was a long hike, but I was back down before anyone knew I had left. I even found a mercury dime about halfway up that trail.

Fishing was the next order of business. Because I had little spare change in those days, I would dig my own worms. I would head to the dam that contained the pond. The water was dirty and I guess fairly deep there. One kid was using cheese rolled into little balls for bait. He was catching one trout after the other. I had limited success with the worms. He offered me some cheese and I started catching trout also. Most were twelve inches or less, but to me they were trophies. His name was Pinky and we immediately became friends. For the week we were there we were inseparable. My parents would see me for meals and bedtime. There was so much to do.

One year we switched it up and decided to go to Calvin Coolidge campground in Vermont where my father had gone when he was a boy.

The campground had lean-tos. Some had magnificent views of the surrounding Green Mountains.

There were numerous streams around and after hearing my father talk of panning for gold when he was little, I eventually talked him into letting me try it, although we never found any gold.

My all-time favorite spot to camp was the Covered Bridge campground in the White Mountains of New Hampshire on the Kangamangus Highway.

The drive took many hours in those days. There was only one way to get there. The route was a winding road that went through mountain passes with waterfalls and crystal clear brooks. The Covered Bridge campground was near the end of the Kangamangus. There was no running water, outhouses and you paid by the honor system. Money was placed into an envelope and dropped into a box. It was a couple dollars for each night you stayed. The campground was nestled in the mountains and the Saco River ran alongside it. Cold and crystal clear, it contained both stocked and native brook trout and rainbows.

There were many signs throughout the campground that warned of bears and the necessity to keep your campsite clean. This was as rustic and pure as my mind could imagine.

Days were spent visiting Santa's Village, Six Gun City and Storyland. I would be given a few dollars to spend at the gift shop. This almost always was spent on some kind of weapon. Slingshots were the choice, but I also recall little cap-guns and bows and arrows. I always pleaded for a pocketknife, but was never allowed one.

I have many fond memories of those years. I had almost forgotten about them until after I separated from the Air Force with a 30 percent disability and the service offered to pay for college. It was during my senior year and I was struggling with a research project to write a thesis. I admired then wildlife biologist Robert Orff. He studied bears and had done many research papers about their habitat and interactions with humans.

I decided to write my paper about the Effects of Natural Food Sources vs. Human Provided on the Black Bears of New Hampshire. I hadn't even seen a bear alive in the woods as a kid. A friend of my father's once brought one home from deer camp. It must have weighed all of 80 pounds. The story goes that the bear was feeding it's way uphill to him while on stand and he shot *at* it several times (7) and hit it twice, once in the foot and lastly at only a few yards away in the face! I do remember seeing one at a garbage can in the Blue Ridge Mountains as a kid while traveling to Georgia. There was cubs involved and many people standing in a circle around them as the cubs fed from the garbage can. My father called it a "disaster waiting to happen"…

So I chose the Covered Bridge campground as my research site. At least I knew there was the possibility of seeing a bear here.

So after school on Friday night I loaded my white Ford pickup with all the essentials…steak, hot dogs and a cooler full of ice cold beer.

I got to the campground after dark and had to take the only spot left next to the outhouses. It was ok once I figured out the prevailing breeze. The tent went up quickly and I settled in for some sleep. Around midnight I awoke to a loud dragging noise and wearily stuck my head out the door of the tent. In the dim light of my flashlight I could see two green eyes illuminated a short distance away and slightly uphill. There were distinct drag marks in the gravel and my cooler lay over on it's side. The culprit quickly departed. My first bear!

The neighboring campsite must have heard all the commotion as a light came on in their tent and I heard a mother and small child as the husband started to unzip the tent. I quietly let them know it might be best to stay inside.

The bear leisurely strolled past my tent and towards the campground road. Not thinking, clad only in my underwear, I gave pursuit. Although I gave the young bear it's distance it paid me no mind. It stopped at the nearest dumpster and deftly lifted the lid and climbed in. After much rustling around it emerged with something in it's mouth and kept on going. It stopped at the outhouse and with the same precision opened the door and went inside. I swear I heard the seat lift and fall back numerous times then out it came and continued on it's way to the next dumpster. The campground road was a large circle and after going the full circumference, the bear found a trail off to one side and departed into the woods. I followed. Even without the use of my flashlight I could see the bear as it was joined by others. They headed further up the trail. We walked for an hour before coming to some rock ledges. It was here that they somehow melted into the landscape and I realized it was getting light. I had a long hike back to the tent.

The next morning I surveyed the damage. My cooler had numerous teeth and claw marks, but was otherwise unscathed. The steak and hot dogs had been consumed. I found five of the six cans of beer. Each had been bitten into and the contents consumed. Well, some party they had last night!

I followed the same trail they had utilized earlier and again came to the ledges. I found no evidence that they had ever been there.

I measured off some food plots and extrapolated the amount of natural forage in those woods from beech and oak trees and extrapolated for the total plot. They certainly had plenty of natural forage available, but obviously the overwhelming urge to partake in human garbage and easy pickings of campers was greater.

On the second night more bears returned and I observed them as they went through their nightly ritual of checking camp sites and the dumpsters. Not one person ever stirred or was aware the bears were or had ever been there that night. I spoke with State Park officials and they said the bears had been doing it for as long as the campground had been open. Sow bears had even been observed bringing their cubs along and teaching them the secrets of the campground smorgasbord!

# OLD MILL POND ROAD

School was finally out for the summer. The first whole week had passed almost uneventful. It was late June and only a few weeks before my birthday. The sun was shining and I had been up early ready for whatever adventure would befall me today. I skipped down the basement stairs and into the garage. It was cool and smelled of motor oil. My father's car was gone as he had left for work even before I was awake.

I reached into the freezer and dug for a green popsicle. I found one and peeled off it's paper wrapper. It emitted a small fog in the already warm day. I placed it in my mouth and headed to the front yard to climb my favorite small white-oak tree. I had nailed boards leading up to the remnants of what was to be my tree house. There was a limb that hung out over the road and I shimmied out until I was over the pavement. Few cars passed by. We lived on a small rural road that made a loop between Route 125 and 111. I think it was Old Mill Pond Road if I remember right...

Looking out from my house the nearest neighbor was across the street. A big white house up on a hill, my Aunt Aggie lived there. I can still picture her kitchen and the homemade doughnuts she would make on Sundays. Further up the road to the right about ¼ mile was my grandfather's country store. I often walked there and he would let me pick out penny candy which I placed in a brown paper sack. Usually I would have most of it eaten before I even got home.

There was a small poodle that lived in a spooky old house just before the store. It always came out and barked and would try to nip at your feet. I once had to utilize my slingshot to protect my younger sister on a walk to the store. The poodle came out as usual and started after my sister. After several attempts to scare the dog away I pulled out my trusty weapon and dispatched the poodle with a smooth white pebble from the side of the road. He never did bother us again.

To the left of my house Old Mill Pond Road traversed a small nameless brook. It was barely noticeable from the road. It was covered over by bushes and ferns. It was dark and mysterious and not quite deep enough to sustain any fish, although my mind often fabricated the possibility of brook and rainbow trout, I fished it numerous times and never caught anything.

Further up the road resided two friends. Randy and Mark. Now Randy was younger than I, but remarkably larger in stature, and Mark was older, yet smaller. He was loud and always ready to do battle at the drop of a hat. I always tried to stay on his good side. Both boys were always dirty and wore ripped jeans and white t-shirts with the sleeves rolled up.

Randy's house was littered with old automobiles, that lay exactly where they had stopped functioning. We often played in these old cars.

Randy also had chickens. There was one rooster that would attack the moment you came around the back of the house. We often had to fend him off with a rake. I thought about my slingshot, but knew Randy would prohibit it.

One time Mark had come strolling to my house. He was on an old tricycle. He was in an particularly bad mood and was challenging me to a game of chicken on tricycles. Our house was in the middle of two hills. You could ride down from both directions and meet at the bottom. He wanted to ride at each other and whomever turned away first would lose.

I declined the challenge and quickly found myself pinned to the ground with Mark on top of me. For a small kid, he weighed a ton!

Randy saved the day by pretending to slap the ground like it was a wrestling match then lifted Mark's arm in the air proclaiming him the winner. At least it got me out from under him without a bloody nose.

Mark wanted more, but Randy distracted him by suggesting we go into the gravel pit behind my house and play. After a minute or two and a brief stare-down, Mark agreed.

The gravel pit was littered with old automobiles. The skeleton of a rusty VW beetle was the first vehicle we came to. Randy had an idea. Perhaps we could roll the VW to the top of the pit and one of us could climb in and then the other two would push it down the wall of the gravel pit.

At the time it seemed like a good idea. I suggested we use the old mattress we found next to it to protect the rider.

Considering it took the three of us, 3 popsicles and half the afternoon to get the VW rolled up the hill, it only took ten seconds for it to tumble down the wall.

It was my first and only car wreck.

# The Yellow Jackets vs. Fruit of The Loom

Many things can distract a boy. It usually begins at an early age. Nothing is more inviting than messing with something that can fight back…snakes for example. They usually don't lend themselves to being caught and often will try to bite if approached, or if you attempt to pick one up. I loved snakes as a kid and would try to catch one if ever I had the chance. Water snakes, Garden snakes, milk snakes, it didn't matter.

But nothing holds more fascination than bees. They can release a world of hurt on you when they sting. They will fiercely defend their hive and swarm in large numbers when they feel threatened. The worker bees will give their lives in defense of the colony.

Occasionally we would come upon a paper wasp nest and throw sticks and rocks at it. Once the wasps came out, we would run. It was exhilarating fun, and often times we were laughing so hard that one of us would actually get stung trying to retreat.

Pinky had spent the night at my house one Friday night. We arose early on Saturday morning and after some discussion of what we would do for the day, it was decided we would build a fort in the woods behind my house.

Pinky had it all figured out. All we would need was a small hatchet and some twine.

"We can cut down some small saplings and lash them to standing trees and build a frame...then attach more until we have a fort built!" he blurted out.

Sounded like it would work to me. I knew where a small hatchet existed and I had a whole roll of twine left over from the last scout camping trip. We were all set.

Pinky led the way.

"Gotta' find the right spot..." he explained.

"Your green-horn woodsman skills would have us building in the middle of a swamp" he further stated.

Across the yard and into the woods we went. Pinky out front and me slightly behind. As we left the sunlight and entered the woods I could smell the pines and decomposing needles on the ground. It got soft underfoot with all those needles. Pinky stopped once and inspected a small stand of saplings. There were four almost in a perfect square shape. He looked to his left and then to his right. As his gaze changed, so did mine. What was he looking at...? He made it quickly apparent.

"These here four trees will be just right to build the framework on. Those small saplings to the right will be perfect to chop down and make into the frame" he remarked, "and those smaller saplings to the left will be just right for filling in the sides and roof...!".

At that moment I understood why he had so quickly been promoted to patrol leader of scout pack 279. It was brilliant.

"Now, I will start cutting down the main poles and you can clear the area between the four trees for us to make into a fort" he huffed, "and do a good job...!"

"ok" was all I could say.

He immediately went to work on cutting a rather large diameter sapling near it's base. I diligently began clearing the space between the four saplings in preparation for the first beam.

After a few minutes of whacking away at the first beam, Pinky hollered to me…"come here, this hatchet is dull, it's gonna' take all day to get this done at this rate…!" he gasped, "why don't you give it a try…?" he said.

I felt honored. Pinky was relinquishing an important job to the likes of me? I could hardly say no. As a matter of fact I was beaming! I practically ran to his side. He handed me the hatchet.

"Now, don't hurt yourself with it" he said, "just start at the base and work your way around it until we can push it…"

He never finished the sentence. I was whacking away at that little tree like it had just bit me and I was retaliating. Pinky later says he'd never seen me so crazed.

"Like you were in some kinda' trance and trying to kill it…" he later said.

The sapling quickly fell to the ground.

"Must have been rotten…" Pinky mumbled under his breath.

"Try this one here" he said, pointing to the next.

I quickly dispatched that one also, and the next twenty-seven, while good old Pinky took a breather on an old stump.

"Wow…!, you got a real knack for that" he said, wiping sweat from his brow.

"Guess we should let you cut all the firewood for camp from here on out" he said. His face was contorted and there was a smirk on his lips.

I took it to be he was impressed. I nodded in agreement.

"You were so good at that, why don't you drag those poles over to the four trees and I will start clearing the ground" he next said.

Of course, I had already cleared it, but maybe it wasn't to his liking. As I struggled with the first one Pinky began pulling at a small clump of something beneath one of those four trees. He was huffing and puffing and really working at it.

"Hey, come help me pull out this scrawny oak" he commanded.

I dropped the pole and went to help. It was about one inch in diameter, but firmly planted in the ground. We dug around it a little. The ground was soft and yielded easily to our effort. Suddenly it became really soft, and our fingers broke into a chamber beneath the soil.

Before Pinky or I could process the thought from brain to speech, two-thousand, mad, yellow-jackets came out from that chamber. We both rolled over backwards, swatting at the fierce attack. There were so many that I couldn't see Pinky two feet away from me. The space between was a black void of angry bees.

Now, I can run, and Pinky wasn't always known for his ability to do anything fast, but all I remember is him dragging me by the arm with yellow jackets all over me stinging me everywhere. I don't remember the bump over the log as we fled. I vaguely remember the dip between the woods and the edge of the lawn. It was here that he let go and we were both in full retreat for my garage. Those angry bees gave chase. We made the corner of the house and promptly made a 90 degree turn.

"Quick...into the garage..!" blurted Pinky.

We made the garage in under three seconds flat and shut the door. Some of the yellow jackets were still on us and we swatted at each other to kill the remaining few. There were painful welts all over our bodies. We had gotten stung in places no one ever wants to get stung!

In the only shaky voice I had ever heard Pinky talk in, he said "that was a close one...!".

"You okay..?" he asked, now recomposing himself.

"I think so" I replied.

We looked at each other and despite our condition began to burst into laughter.

"You wanna' go back and teach 'em a lesson?" Pinky queried.

It had crossed my mind, but I simply said "not today---maybe another day---now we know where they are..." I replied.

"Yeah, good idea" said Pinky.

We laughed again. It was then that we realized some of the survivors were still underneath our clothing. A few had made their way into my fruit-of-the-looms. I tried desperately to swat at them, but realized I would have to take them off. Pinky seemed to be afflicted with the same problem, and quickly removed his also. Now was not the time for vanity.

It was about then that my mother appeared. Our backs were to her when she said;

"What are you boys up to...?"

The words had barely escaped her lips when we turned in embarrassment. Her jaw dropped in horror. Our bodies were covered in red, swollen welts from head to toe. It must have looked awful. She didn't even take notice of us being sans clothing.

"Oh my god...!", "what happened to you two?" she questioned. Her face was now gentle---like when I had begged for my first puppy.

"Oh, you know, building a fort in the woods...it was really coming along until we found a yellow jacket nest right where we wanted to build it" I answered.

Pinky was cringing. The welts were now starting to hurt and I don't think he wanted either me or my mother to see that he was in discomfort. We both were hopping up and down, writhing with pain.

"Pritchard, are you alright?" my mother asked.

"Uh...why yes Mrs. Bingel" he replied.

Squirming, he couldn't stand still any longer. Nor could I. The hopping became more pronounced. In retrospect, it was quite funny.

My mom did her best to coat us with calamine lotion. She called the family doctor and Pinky's mom.

Pinky and I got a little delirious from all those stings, but it didn't stop us from going back later that day to tempt fate yet again and let those yellow jackets know we weren't two to be messed with...I did throw away those Fruit-of-the-loom underwear---just in case...